Fine WoodWorking
Biennial Design Book

Fine WoodWorking Biennial Design Book

Compiled and Edited by the
Editors of Fine Woodworking Magazine

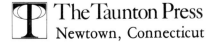
The Taunton Press
Newtown, Connecticut

Cover photographs:

THOMAS N. BERGER (top left and p. 22)
Ringoes, N. J.
Detail: rocker

PATRICK ROBBINS (top right and p. 118)
Pontiac, Mich.
Detail: portrait of Carol; self-portrait

DARRELL De RUITER (bottom left)
White Cloud, Mich.
Detail: sculptural form
Birch burl, pine
72 high

ROBERT W. BAILEY (bottom right and p. 115)
Woodleaf, N. C.
Detail: chest on chest

Book Designer: Roger Barnes

Typeface: Compugraphic Garamond 9 point—Text
        Caslon 540—Display

Paper: Mead Offset Enamel 70 lb.—Text
       International Feedcote 12 point—Cover

Printer: Connecticut Printers, Bloomfield, Conn.

First printing: June 1977
Second printing: October 1977
Third printing: April 1978

The Taunton Press, Inc.
52 Church Hill Road
Box 355
Newtown, Connecticut 06470

International Standard Book Number 0-918804-00-0
Library of Congress Catalog Card Number 77-79327
Printed in the United States of America

Contents

Introduction

This is a book of 600 photographs of 500 designs by 440 woodworkers, the pick of 8,000 photographs sent to *Fine Woodworking* magazine by about 1,200 designer-craftsmen from all over North America.

When the photos were sorted and cataloged and numbered, the editors of *Fine Woodworking* met to ''do'' the book. We began by confessing our doubts about the wisdom of attempting to judge woodworking from photos, without being able to see and touch the wood itself. Obviously we could not, so our challenge really was to edit a large collection of photographs into a book. Our criteria were good design, attractive use of wood, unity of conception and detailing, and attention to the principles of wooden construction. Our aim was to show the state of the art in all its diversity—from antique interpretations to ultramodern fantasies.

To accomplish this, the photographs and color slides were divided by function into 53 groups. They were sorted according to style and construction, so we could compare like with like and view them in coherent groups. We selected the things we all liked, rejected blurry or bad photographs, and pondered what remained. The general category ''tables and desks,'' for example, contained more than 1,000 photos at the start, and we chose fewer than 100. ''Musical instruments,'' on the other hand, had fewer than 50 to start. The whole collection of 8,000 photographs was sifted twice more during the actual editing of the book.

Changes in time are reflected by changes in both function and style. The salt boxes and dry sinks of yesteryear are the coffee tables and stereo cabinets of today. And the sculptured forms being created by today's designers are no further removed from ''modern'' furniture developed earlier in this century than the highly sculptured Queen Anne was from its Jacobean predecessors.

Most of the work in this book is contemporary, a reflection of the entries we received. But the continuous thread of classical cabinet-making—especially from the 18th century—can be seen on every page of this book, for that, after all, is the heritage of the contemporary designer.

Much contemporary woodworking is influenced by the idea that furniture can also be sculpture. If function is only one aspect of form, new forms can be explored that still serve the old functions. However, wood is still the most convenient material, even though the resulting piece of furniture might as well be made of plastic. . . or ferroconcrete.

Until quite recently, wood was not only the preferred material, it was the only material. It was nature's plastic, and it was filled, stained, inlaid, gilded or ebonized to look the way the designers wanted it to look.

Today there are plastics and metals and glass, not to mention chipboard and other wood by-products, all readily fashioned by contemporary technology. The designer who doesn't want the figure and texture of wood can use plastic. Or if a wood joint is too bulky, one can weld steel.

On the other hand, a contemporary designer who works in wood has *chosen* to do so. The wood is to *be* wood. Peculiar twists of grain or rare changes in color—defects the factory would reject and the ancestor would cover with stain—are often sought. In much contemporary woodworking these singularities have become the main thing. Indeed, a piece of furniture may be designed and built to feature an unusual piece of wood.

Woodworkers sometimes note that a tree is about as tough as a person, and it is about all a lone person can do to transform a tree into a cabinet. In the process, the wood will also transform the maker. Trees are to the vegetable kingdom what people are to the animal kingdom, a fair match.

A person walking in the woods or along the shore is apt to pick up a stick, break it to length, snap off the twigs, tidy the bark. This is basic woodworking. Walk with the new stick, poke things with it, hit some rocks. This is the first tool. But naked wood isn't much more durable than flesh. Few ancient artifacts of wood have survived, which is probably why the Stone Age is considered so important. But the Wood Age must have come first, and is still with us. Wood is our favorite material, so much so that we try to make acres of plastic laminate look just like it.

It's a long way from sticks to elegant bentwood chairs, although just a few centuries ago, chairs were so scarce that only the *chair*man had one. For the craftsman working alone, machines have made the preparatory work much less difficult and tedious, but the really hard tasks of designing and joining and finishing are still done by hand. After the thing has been made once, the factory can make a million exactly like it. And earlier in this century it seemed sufficient to have just copies. The designer-craftsman almost became extinct. This is changing today and one may suggest dozens of reasons why. But the fact is, one can study woodworking and furniture design at the college level in nearly every state. A multitude of young people are attempting to make a career of being designer-craftsmen. And many more thousands of amateurs are gracing their homes with pieces they have designed and built. This book documents their achievements, but only hints at the thousands of hours they spent to achieve these graceful designs.

This book represents a great deal of work by the staff of *Fine Woodworking* magazine, but especially by Vivian Dorman, who shepherded the project and kept track of all the many photos, letters and odd bits of paper, and by Roger Barnes, who designed the book.

On each page, the captions refer to photographs in a left-to-right order. The dimensions are in inches. The comments in italic type are by the makers of the pieces and follow the information about the photograph. They were excerpted from the letters that accompanied many of the entries.

We entitled this ''Biennial Design Book'' because we intend to do it again in two years. Designer-craftsmen, amateur or professional, are invited to send entries of their best work done in 1977 and 1978, and should write for full details from The Taunton Press.

Newtown, Conn.
May 12, 1977

Tage Frid
R. Bruce Hoadley
John Kelsey
Paul Roman

Architecture

VICTOR J. MULLAN (overleaf)
Baltimore, Md.
Detail: kitchen wall
Wormy chestnut
114 x 180

GORDON HULSE
Staten Island, N.Y.
Wall unit
Cherry, teak
110 x 96 x 22

RIC PULS
Elkhart Lake, Wis.
Window
Oak, walnut, German crackled glass,
stained glass
30 dia.; $550

Sun window
Oak, walnut
36 x 48; $900

"My real interest is windows with
stained and beveled glass. I depart
from traditional methods by using
wood instead of lead to hold the glass.
Were the glass clear the window could
stand on its own merit. I use only the
natural colors of the woods to contrast
with each other."

10

HOLGER M. LAUBMEIER
Del Mar, Calif.
Double doors
White oak, black walnut,
ribbon-grain mahogany
96 x 66 x 2

*"The L-shaped branch below the lock
comes away from the oak to serve
as a handle."*

JAY JOHNSON
Kansas City, Mo.
Cabinet with built-in desk
Black walnut
107 x 83 x 11

PHILLIP DIAL
Houston, Tex.
Entrance to a club
Cedar, mahogany, parana, oak,
redwood, clear white pine
60 x 144; $3,000

*"It was so contrived to have a
directional pull to the front entrance of
the club, which was not easily seen
from the street."*

WOODGRAIN'RY
Cambridge, Mass.
*Coffee Connection II in the Faneuil
Hall Marketplace, Boston, Mass.*
Red oak
Photo by V. L. Gozbekian

*"...designed by Woodgrain'ry with
George Howell, owner of the store."*

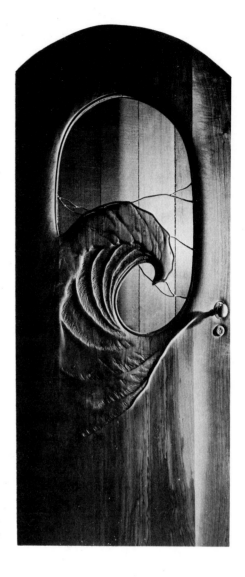

JAMES SANDBERG
Albion, Calif.
Dolphin door
Black walnut, German hand-blown
stained glass
84 x 36 x 3
Photos by Judith Brown and
Peter Dobbins

DENNIS STROH
Denver, Colo.
Stairway rail
Red oak
55 ft. long

*"The rail is made of laminated red
oak. The pieces were not steamed, but
glued up and then clamped
into forms."*

BRIAN SCOTT
McKinleyville, Calif.
Door
Douglas fir, redwood, white oak
84 x 40 x 4
Photo by Alan Olmstead

*"Its fabrication consists of a series of
laminations. The core is solid,
1-1/2-in. Douglar fir, next a 1/2-in.
layer of clear and in areas parqueted
curly redwood. Finally the relief design
is in 3/4-in. white oak . . . the oak
design itself is let into the redwood
and is attached to the core."*

KIT ANDREWSON
Bolinas, Calif.
Scarab
Redwood
$500

 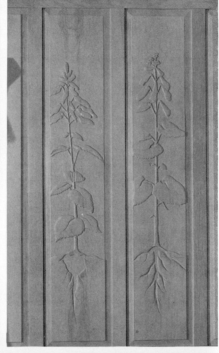

D. H. MEIKLEM
Yantic, Conn.
Bedroom and accessories
Chair and table, maple; wall, clear
pine, pickled white

DAVID TROE
Brighton, Mass.
Door and screen
Door: cherry, maple veneer; screen:
cherry, maple and walnut laminations,
padauk
84 x 36; $1,000

JOHN WARD
Santa Rosa, Calif.
Clock tower

*"No paint was used and only a few
small details were darkened
with stain."*

JAWAR
Taos, N. Mex.
Curvilaminar I
Mahogany, walnut, red oak
78 x 42 x 2-1/2

Burst
Mahogany
78 x 36 x 2-1/4

*"The doors are a mosaic technique I
originated, with individual pieces
splined to all others."*

RANDY MORGAN
Laguna Beach, Calif.
Tribute Gauguin, carved door
Alder
84 x 36; $4,000

*"This carving was inspired by Paul
Gauguin who is my favorite painter."*

ROBERT W. MELZER
Telluride, Colo.
Kitchen cabinets
Birch, tigerwood, rosewood, angico,
mahogany, walnut, vermilion
144 long
Photo by Donna J. Faulkner

JOHN WALL
Warren, Vt.
Front door
South American walnut, koa,
blown rondel windows
80 x 36 x 4

JOHN BICKEL
Ossining, N.Y.
Interior cabinets
Philippine mahogany plywood,
Philippine mahogany

*"...for built-in tuner, phonograph
turntable, tape deck, speakers,
storage and seating."*

EDWARD M. LEVIN
Canaan, N.H.
Hammer-beam roof for blacksmith shop
Spruce
22 ft. x 31 ft.

M. ROBERT VAN ARSDALE
San Cristobal, N. Mex.
Dragon door
Honduras mahogany, cherry, walnut
80 x 32

Mayan door (Quetzalcoatl)
Black walnut
96 x 40
Photos by Tony Holmes

RODNEY CULVER HILL and
SUSAN MILLER HILL
College Station, Tex.
Panels for Texas A & M University
100-year history
Walnut
36 x 96 each

"...the panels touch upon virtually
every aspect of the university's
heritage, including the beginning
landmarks of the campus, a composite
of uniforms worn by A&M's Corps of
Cadets since 1876, sports and
traditions, and the varied
academic programs."

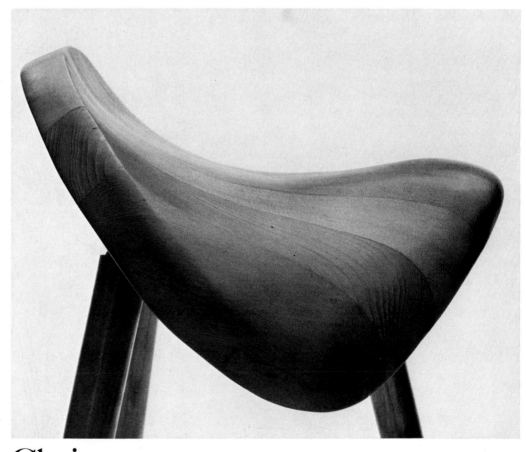

Chairs

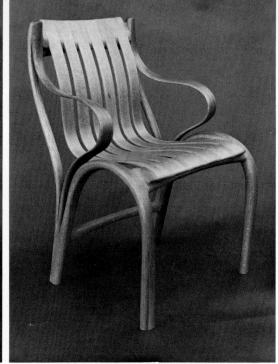

ROBSON SPLANE, JR. (overleaf)
Northridge, Calif.
Detail: three-legged stool
Redwood, cherry

RONNIE PUCKETT
Providence, R.I.
Chair
Maple, cotton velvet
33 x 24 x 20; $1,200 for four

WILLIAM PARSONS
Richmond, Va.
Arm chair
White oak, strip laminated
33 x 20 x 20

JERE OSGOOD
New Milford, Conn.
Desk chair
Rosewood

THOMAS N. BERGER
Ringoes, N.J.
(Interpretive) Shaker rocker
Vermont black cherry, black walnut,
white oak, sapling hickory splints,
maple joints
42 x 21 x 19

*"I work a great deal with Shaker
attitudes: simplicity, functionality,
delicateness, unpretentious but with a
quiet, built-in strength. The Shakers
enjoyed looking at the inherent beauty
of grain patterns, textures and colors
and had enough sense to use
hardwoods instead of pine. It is
important to take the time to learn the
qualities and characteristics of the
woods we use."*

JAMES SCHRIBER
Allston, Mass.
Side chair
Bubinga, blue suede
34 x 16 x 17; $375

TIMOTHY PHILBRICK
Boston, Mass.
Desk chair
Maple
38 x 17-1/4 x 15

22

THOMAS L. CLARK
Columbus, Ohio
*Philadelphia type Chippendale
armchair*
So. American mahogany, pine
redwood
39 x 32 (wide)

*"Mortise and tenon throughout;
made from rough sawn stuff entirely
with hand tools of period type."*

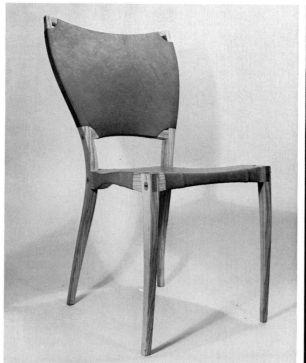

JOHN FOSSUM
Allston, Mass.
Chair
Ash, leather
37 x 18 x 17-1/2 ; $500

NATHAN ROME
Cambridge, Mass.
Rocker
Oak
42 x 26 x 34

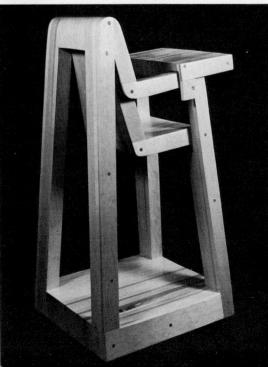

JOHN DODD
Rochester, N.Y.
Lounge chair
Oak
32 x 22 x 27

JAMES LIDDELL, designer;
GEORGE G. OLIVE, maker
Austin, Tex.
High chair
Southern white pine
38 x 18 x 20
Photo by S. Gillies

24

STEPHEN R. MOORE
Pleasantville, N.Y.
Dining chair
Red oak
42 high; $625

*"The finished chair
weighs approximately five pounds
There is only the slightest give even
with the heaviest people."*

ROBERT MARCH
Rochester, N.Y.
Armchair
Oak
48 x 25 x 24; $800

JEFFREY R. ALL
Terre Haute, Ind.
Subtle rocker
White oak
31 x 45 x 18
Photo by Bob Lance

WILLIAM B. DUNN
Lee, Mass.
Rocker
Walnut, jute twine

*"All curved pieces are laminated. The
chair is based upon the dimensions and
curves of a Boston rocker."*

GEORGE H. KAUB
Denver, Colo.
*Twist-turned chair—circa. 1870,
American*
Cherry
40 x 13 x 13

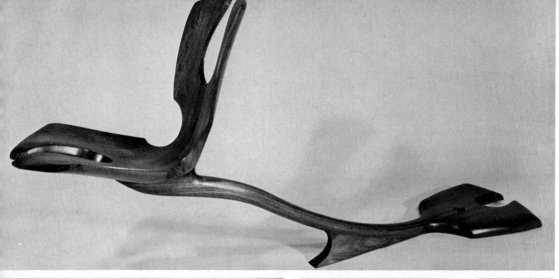

C. R. JOHNSON
Stoughton, Wis.
Springer #2
Walnut
32 x 17 x 60

"Lag-bolted to floor at the pad and yet can pivot around bolt. Springer made of 3/16 x 2 x 72 laminations."

PAUL CUSACK
Philadelphia, Pa.
Spindle back rocker
Mahogany, cane
48 x 20 x 36; $500

THOS. MOSER
New Gloucester, Maine
Continuous arm Windsor chair (patent pending)
Cherry, ash, maple
$240

KAREN STRAUS
Barrington, N.J.
Rocking chair
Walnut, cherry, imbuya
48 x 30 x 20; $2,000

MICHAL ROSEN
Westfield, N.J.
Dining or desk chair
Black walnut
30 x 20 (wide); $225

"Back swivels 360°."

STEVE LEVINSON
Westford, Vt.
Throne chair
Vermont cherry
67 x 37-1/2 x 34

*"Commissioned by Buddhist
Meditation Center; for use by visiting
teacher and designed to be sat on by an
exceptionally heavy individual."*

JOHN PETERSON
Brookline, Mass.
Side chair
Pear
35-1/4 x 15-3/4 x 18;
seat 16-3/4; $315

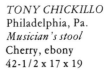

TONY CHICKILLO
Philadelphia, Pa.
Musician's stool
Cherry, ebony
42-1/2 x 17 x 19

"Designed for performing violinist or double bass player."

BRADLEY V. SMITH
San Diego, Calif.
Plant stand
Walnut
25 x 10 x 11; $180

© *DAISY SCHNEPEL*
Foster, R.I.
Strung chairs
Cherry, walnut, nylon/dacron cord
31-1/2 x 26-3/4 x 34
cherry, $175; walnut, $190

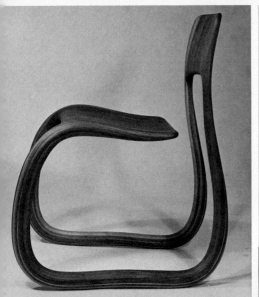

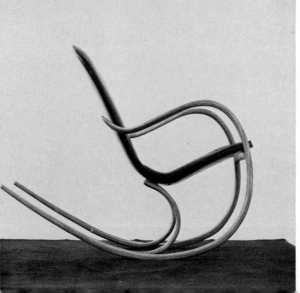

© *DAVID FLATT 1976*
Belleville, Wis.
Cantilever chair
Walnut, laminated
30 x 18 x 23; $395

FRANK J. BECHT
Buffalo, N.Y.
Rocker
Red oak, cowhide
25 x 23 x 32; $375

RON NELSON
Anoka, Minn.
Swede rocker
Ponderosa pine
36 x 23 x 28; $1,500

*"I glue up a block of pine in roughly
the shape I want and then carve it,
beginning with chain saw and ending
with carving tools."*

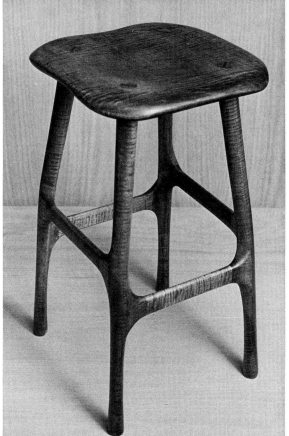

DEAN TORGES &
JACK GUTILLA
Ostrander, Ohio
Sculpted stool
Curly maple
22-1/2 x 12-5/8 x 12-5/8

*"We work together, cut the trees that
we use together, and scratch out livings
for our families together doing what
we love most."*

CHRISTOPHER MURRAY
Richmond, Va.
Stool
41 x 16 x 14; $350

WILL ORVEDAL
Lawrence, Kans.
Rocker
Walnut, cherry
26 x 40; $250

JOHN F. ASTELL
Madison, Wis.
Horse stool
Red oak
16 high

"I grew up on a farm and the horse
stool expresses my rural background.
Chisel marks create a hairy feeling. The
haunches at the rear of the seat lend
great posterior support. It's the most
comfortable stool I've ever sat upon."

TIM MACKANESS
Portland, Ore.
Dining chicken chair
Black walnut, koa
39 x 21 x 26
Photo by Craig Hickman

JAMES L. HENKLE
Norman, Okla.
Folding stool
Beech
18 x 18 x 18; $300

TOM WESSELLS
Newport News, Va.
Rocker
White oak, Nicaraguan rosewood
36 x 24 x 40; $1,000

*"All of the elements of this piece are
laminated with the exception of the
bars on the front of the seat and top
of the back."*

THOM HUCKER
Brookline, Mass.
Side chair
Maple
40 x 18 (wide); $650

*"Laminated and staved seat
construction, the back legs are double
tapered (each laminate stripe) and
then laminated to the curve so no
laminates are cut through."*

PAUL J. HECHT
New Rochelle, N.Y.
Molded veneer rocker
Cherry, ebony, cane
43 x 24 x 43

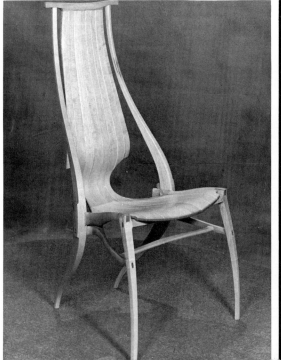
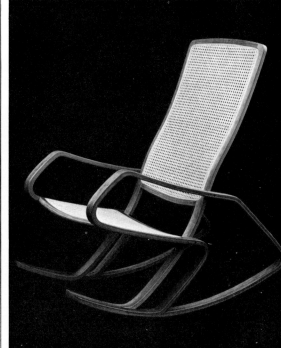

31

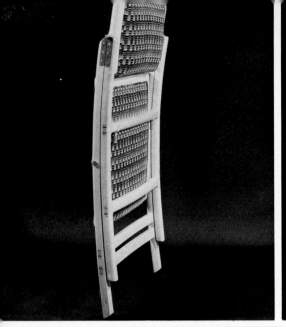

ROSANNE SOMERSON
Belmont, Mass.
Upholstered folding chair
Laminated maple, velveteen, pirelli
webbing, dacron & foam, handmade
brass & steel fittings
folded: 35 x 19 x 3

CHRISTOPHER L. WEILAND
Rochester, N.Y.
Chair
Cherry, hickory
54 high

DAVID M. GROSZ
Mt. Vernon, N.Y.
Chair
Sycamore, apple, curly maple,
mahogany, ash, gum, walnut,
ebony, padauk, deerskin, bronze,
brass, steel
84 wingspan

E.E. "SKIP" BENSON
San Francisco, Calif.
Reading chair
Cherry, kid upholstery, down
filled
42 x 28 x 36

JOHN DUNNIGAN
Saunderstown, R.I.
Ladderback chair
Cherry
48 x 18 x 16; $175

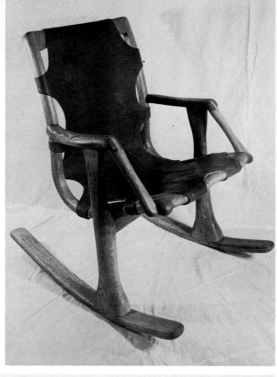

RICHARD RANGELL
Carmel, Calif.
Rocker
Walnut, leather
38 x 25 x 19
Photo by Tony Grant

NORMAN R. DOLL
Madison, Wis.
Rocker-type #1
Red oak, leather
36 x 25 x 33

ALAN FRIEDMAN
Terre Haute, Ind.
Rocker
Philippine mahogany
31-1/2 x 18 x 48

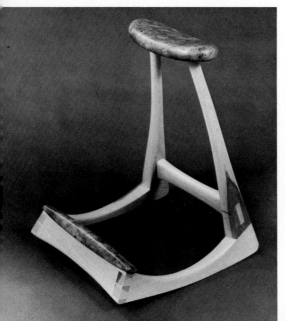

BRADFORD SMITH
Rochester, N.Y.
Rocking stool
Hickory, elm burl
26 x 18 x 22

STEVEN A. FOLEY
Lake Oswego, Ore.
Bentwood chair
Oregon white oak
27 x 22 x 21; $650

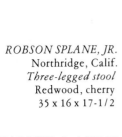

ROBSON SPLANE, JR.
Northridge, Calif.
Three-legged stool
Redwood, cherry
35 x 16 x 17-1/2

BRADFORD C. deWOLF
McLean, Va.
Armchair
Walnut, oak

"My wife collaborates by doing the needlepoint seats."

WILLIAM C. LEETE
Marquette, Mich.
Cantilevered chair
Laminated ash, leather
47 x 24 x 42; $936

ALAN FRIEDMAN
Terre Haute, Ind.
Occasional chair
Plywood
30-1/2 x 20-1/4

ELLEN SWARTZ
Rochester, N.Y.
Armchair
Plywood
21 x 22 x 32

THOMAS DEADY
Maple Valley, Wash.
Chair
Laminated walnut
46 x 24 x 21

TIM CROWDER
San Diego, Calif.
Wishbone rocker
Oak
Photo by J. Ahrend

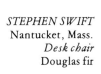

STEPHEN SWIFT
Nantucket, Mass.
Desk chair
Douglas fir

ROBERT CHEHAYL
Westfield, N.J.
Chair
Walnut, steam bent
33 x 23 x 22

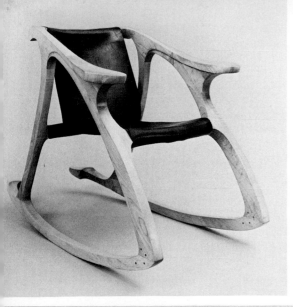

ROBERT STEINBERG
Philadelphia, Pa.
Rocker
Maple, leather
31 x 25 x 42

CHARLES J. MARINO
Pueblo, Colo.
Chair
Teakwood
30 x 15-3/4; seat 15-1/4

ALPHONSE MATTIA
Belmont, Mass.
Rocker
Vermilion, cotton velvet over down
48 x 30 x 48

JACK TAYLOR III
De Kalb, Ill.
Dining chair
Hickory
35 x 20; arm 27

BRUCE BEEKEN
North Ferrisburg, Vt.
Side chair
Maple, leather
31 x 17 x 16-1/2, seat 17

"Offset turned legs, laminated rails, back."

H. SCOTT HERMAN
New Haven, Conn.
Chair
Black walnut, laminated and
carved
48 x 24 x 24

*"Designed for a female between
5-foot-2 and 5-foot-8."*

JIM HABER
Silver Spring, Md.
Stool
Oak, mahogany, cherry
28 x 14 x 14
Photo by Richard Folkers

*"Designed and built to match my
workbench, the stool, except for two
small pieces of mahogany and two
small pieces of cherry which are glued
into the seat, is made entirely of oak
reclaimed from old skids finished with
three coats of Deft."*

PHILIP C. STRANGE
Woodberry Forest, Va.
Folding chair
Walnut, ash
open-27 x 16 (wide);
closed-31 x 6-1/2; $175

*"Both the front and back legs were
laminated on the same jig. This is so
the legs will fit snugly when the chair
is folded. The slats in the seat fit
into a groove on both sides of the seat
frame. Slats were used to allow room
for expansion and contraction
in the wood."*

SCOTT DICKERSON
Brooksville, Maine
Dining chair
Cherry, natural cane
38 x 22 x 18; $225
Photo by David Klopferstein

JAMES D. NASH
Anaheim, Calif.
Swing chair
Koa
68 high

DAVID N. EBNER
Brookhaven, N.Y.
Rocker
Laminated oak, cane
31 x 30 x 24; $1,000

ROGER DEATHERAGE
Houston, Tex.
Rocker
Ash, hickory, leather
43 x 26 x 35; $950

JON KUHN
Richmond, Va.
Cantilevered chair
Ash
30 x 27-1/2 x 43; $1,250
Photo by Melissa Grimes

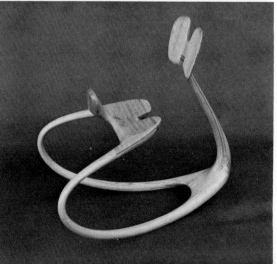

LEONARD JACOBS
Los Angeles, Calif.
Rocker
Walnut, cowhide
34 x 25 x 36

WILLIAM HAMMERSLEY
Richmond, Va.
Ash rocking stool
Laminated ash
30 x 35 x 26; $400

NORBERT MARKLIN
St. Louis, Mo.
Sand rocker
White oak, red oak, walnut

*"Sand compartment in bottom front.
Sand adjusts to each person's weight
by flowing into 1 of 3 inner chambers.
Two walnut bumpers keep chair
from overextending."*

ROBERT L. DOMLESKY
Charlemont, Mass.
Rocker
Walnut
44 x 48 x 24

*"Rockers laminated; back spindles
steam bent."*

GUY RING
Beverly Hills, Calif.
Rocker
Teak, aluminum
44 x 30 x 30

*"The rockers themselves are
aluminum with a 1/8-in. thick layer of
teak laminated to the top and
bottom surface."*

Tables and Desks

JOHN W. McNAUGHTON (overleaf)
Evansville, Ind.
Detail: chain table
Walnut, zebrawood
$400

W. A. KEYSER, JR.
Rush, N.Y.
Coffee table
Walnut
17 x 36 x 60

MARK LEACH
Providence, R.I.
End tables/coffee table
Cherry
each, 20 x 25 x 17; $4,000

MARK HIGGISON
Philadelphia, Pa.
Tambour desk
White oak, black walnut
42 x 37 x 28

MARV PALLISCHECK
Fairport, N.Y.
End table
Red oak
17-1/2 x 26 x 15-1/4
Photo by Paul Wiedrich

TOM F. URBAN
Eugene, Ore.
Peanut table
Red oak
30 high, 40 long; $800
Photo by Jim Bourdin

J. KELLY CONKLIN
Rochester, N.Y.
Slate and maple table
47 x 23-1/2 x 21-1/2 ; $625

WILLIAM PARSONS
Richmond, Va.
Roll-top desk
White oak with walnut interior
48 x 36 x 20 ; $925

STEPHEN SWIFT
Nantucket, Mass.
Secretary desk
Black walnut, African mahogany
72 x 30 x 18 ; $675

DAVID M. GROSZ
Mt. Vernon, N.Y.
Desk
Pecan, hickory
30 x 30 x 84 ; $1,200

KINGSLEY C. BROOKS
Cambridge, Mass.
Candlestand
Ash
26 high, 17 dia. ; $125

JAMES G. VASI
Buffalo, N.Y.
Stacking Tables
Walnut
18 x 18; $150

ROBERT A. SCHULTZ
Appleton, Wis.
Table
Walnut
20 x 17 x 24

AL HANCOCK
Utica, Ky.
Comtemporary table
American black walnut
18-1/2 x 14 x 23-1/2 (glass, 26 x 34)

"The rails are doweled in the legs."

MARK SFIRRI
Foster, R.I.
Writing desk
Cherry
30 x 48 x 50

KEN STRICKLAND
Croton-on-Hudson, N.Y.
Chair with a desk
Ash, maple veneer
18 x 24 x 33; $650

TOM ECKERT
Tempe, Ariz.
Oak table
Laminated white oak, white oak veneer
17-1/2 x 18 x 46; $500

ACORN WOODWORKS
Tucson, Ariz.
Dining table
Shedua, wenge, bubinga, padauk,
imbuya
36 x 50 dia. (78 long with extensions)

*"Legs of table penetrate top and
transform into functional items, i. e.
salad bowl, salad servers, candle
holders, salt and pepper grinder, wine
decanter, oil and vinegar containers."*

DAVID E. WINER
Washington, D.C.
Drop-leaf dining table
Black cherry heartwood with sapwood
accents
42 x 84

SANDY BRENNER
Scottsville, N.Y.
Coffee table
Walnut
15-1/2 x 15-1/2 x 48; $300

ANDREW PEKLO III
Southbury, Conn.
Stacking tables
Shedua
13 x 13 x 22; $225

ERIK GRONBORG
Solana Beach, Calif.
Scrooge's desk
Avocado wood
48 high, 39 wide

T. H. WEATHERILL
Kansas City, Mo.
Table
Koa
open, 30 x 20 x 50; $450

ROBERT FREEMAN
Newton Center, Mass.
Backgammon table and box
Oak and walnut plywood, rosewood,
satinwood and mahogany veneer
28-3/4 x 30 x 30

JOE TRACY
Somesville, Maine
Backgammon table
Cherry, pear, walnut
27 x 27-1/4 x 31-1/4; $500

DAVID C. GOSS
Columbus, Ohio
Chippendale piecrust table
Honduras mahogany
28-1/4 high x 32 dia.

ROBERT R. JORGENSEN
Denver, Colo.
Wall desk
Walnut
54 x 23 x 60; $935

DICK LOUGHLIN
Jensen Beach, Fla.
Coffee table
3/4-in. birch plywood, walnut veneer
with rosewood top insert
36-3/4 x 36-3/4 x 15
Photo by Conant Photo Shop & Studio

H. L. LeCOMPTE, JR.
Towson, Md.
Hepplewhite board
Mahogany
39 x 24 x 62-1/2

JOSEPH MULLAN, maker;
LINDA HARDER, designer
Baltimore, Md.
Secretary
Walnut, rosewood, myrtle
82 x 41 x 22; $24,000

DANIEL MEYERSON
Philadelphia, Pa.
Dining table
Cherry
29 x 40 x 60 (closed); 78 long (open)
$900

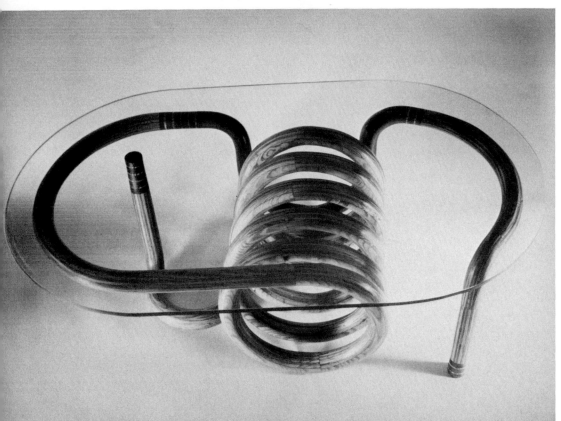

JOHN W. McNAUGHTON
Evansville, Ind.
Spring table
C/D plywood, walnut
$400

Hanging table
C/D plywood, walnut
$400

"All projects constructed of totally separate but interdependent elements which allows each table to be dismantled and reassembled into another form of table or arranged purely as sculpture. The thesis that furniture and sculpture are interchangeable has dominated my work for the past 2 years."

N. L. WHITE
Rochester, N.Y.
Modular tables
Chilean laurel burl over ply armature
18 x 27 x 24; $800 pr.

SOLID WOOD
Omaha, Nebr.
Poudre Canyon wine cart
Pine
36-1/4 x 21-1/8 x 30; $395

TOM SIMONS
Santa Fe, N. Mex.
Trestle table
American black walnut
120 x 48

*"My adaptation of the traditional
trestle table and a more organic
unsettling element in the vines."*

DAVID BOOKBINDER
Mayfield Village, Ohio
French provincial serving table
Maple, zebrawood
26 x 18 x 29

"The top is structured of 129 pieces, arranged in a marquetry design to simulate an optical illusion of three-dimensional cubes."

KATHRYN WAITE SCHACKNER
Rochester, N.Y.
Inlaid glass-topped table
Cherry, imbuya, padauk, satinwood, poplar
29 x 16 x 48

GERALD C. NASH
Santa Monica, Calif.
Display pedestals
Birch
18-1/2 high, 8 dia. (largest)
Photo by Erik Nash

RONNIE PUCKETT
Providence, R.I.
Writing table
Madeira, fiddleback mahogany
40 x 40 x 20

JOHN BETTS
Champaign, Ill.
Extension/gaming table
Birch plywood, walnut
27-3/4 x 36 x 36 (closed)

DAVID P. FULLER
Chatham, N.Y.
Chinese table
Teak, oak
33 x 39 x 21; $540
Photo by Christian Steiner

PORTER E. LITTLEFIELD
Philadelphia, Pa.
Extension table
White oak
29 x 35 x 58

REED M. HODGDON
Westerville, Ohio
Mule-foot table
Honduras mahogany
18-1/4 x 15-1/4 23-3/4
Photo by Steve Liao

MEG RODGERS
Philadelphia, Pa.
Folding table and benches
Birch, mahogany
29 x 36 x 65 dia. (table)
Photo by Eugene Mopsik

SCOTT CHIPMAN
San Diego, Calif.
Folding table
Elm
36 x 36 x 28

ALAN C. MARKS
Pacific Grove, Calif.
Meditation stool
Ash, elm
5 x 15-3/4 x 11-3/4; $300

GARY LOGSTED
Chester, N.J.
Coffee table
Cherry, maple, walnut
15 x 28 x 37; $300

RICHARD KAGAN
Philadelphia, Pa.
Elliptical coffee table
Zebrawood
27-1/4 x 13 x 55-1/2; $625

TIM MACKANESS
Portland, Ore.
Tree frog foot table II
Black walnut
24 x 24 x 26
Photo by Craig Hickman

*"My constructions in wood evolve
through experiments in clay. From a
clay model, I make a silhouette or
projection and enlarge it into a life-size
cartoon that allows me to calculate the
dimensions, joinery and laminations
required to construct the final piece
with a minimum of waste."*

KONRAD M. RICHTER, JR.
Westmont, N.J.
Book stand
Cherry
12 x 18 x 18; $285

CHARLES J. SANDERS
Pueblo, Colo.
Writing desk
Cherry
46 x 36 x 13
Photo by Kerry Peterson

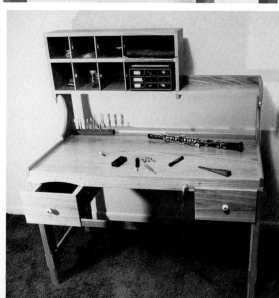

D. N. LAMONT
Billings, Mont.
Bench for making oboe reeds
Solid red oak
53 x 48 x 24

MARK S. LEVIN
Evanston, Ill.
Coffee table
Walnut
48 x 48 x 16; $1,750

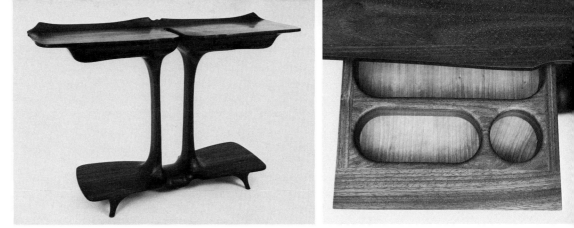

ED DADEY
Marquette, Nebr.
Hunt table
Vermilion
36 x 18 x 54

JOHN KENNEDY
Philadelphia, Pa.
Dining-room extension table
Walnut
30 x 44 x 68 (82 open)

JONATHAN WRIGHT
Florence, Mass.
Coffee table
American black walnut
13 x 26 x 42
Photo by Robert Lyons Photography

KIP NEALE
Housatonic, Mass.
Drafting table
American black walnut, boxwood
30-40 x 36 x 54; $800
Photo by Wendy Pollock

*"Table height can be adjusted in 2-in.
increments from 30 in. to 40 in.; tilt of
top is 35° in each direction."*

DONALD LLOYD McKINLEY
Mississauga, Ontario, Canada
Reception desk
Bent laminated form, walnut veneer,
3/4-in. smoked glass
75 long

MICHAEL CIARDELLI
Milford, N.H.
Trestle table
Black walnut
30 x 36 x 116

60

DAVID W. LAMB
Canterbury, N.H.
Desk on frame
Cherry, eastern white pine
44-1/2 x 33-1/2 x 20; $2,700

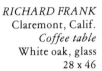

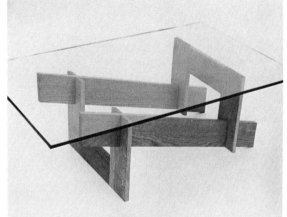

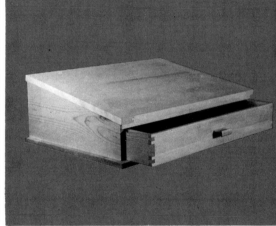

RICHARD FRANK
Claremont, Calif.
Coffee table
White oak, glass
28 x 46

DANIEL SCHAFFHAUSER
Severna Park, Md.
Bench desk
White pine, basswood
6 x 23-1/2 x 17-1/4

EDWIN KRALES
New York, N.Y.
Set of living-room tables
American walnut, African
mahogany inlay
Large table, 17 x 24 x 72;
smallest, 24 x 18 x 24

*"Each leg and top has eight inlays—a
total of 40 inlays per table."*

ROBERT DONOVAN
Worcester, Mass.
Tavern table
Walnut
27 x 15 x 35

"The solid top is sculptured. The rear of the table design is the same as the front."

ROBERT MARCH
Rochester, N.Y.
Side table
Rosewood
30 x 16 x 60; $1,300

PETER HOEFER
San Francisco, Calif.
Reading table
Black walnut
33 x 34 x 23

KEN WILLIS
Glen Allen, Va.
Writing table
Walnut
30-1/2 x 31-1/2 x 57

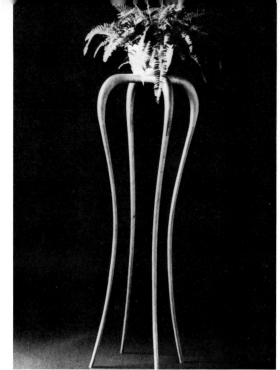

MARK S. LEVIN
Evanston, Ill.
Plant stand
Cherry, walnut
48 x 16 x 16; $750

F. E. GLAWSON
Wilmington, Calif.
Flower vase stand
Walnut, oak burl
24 high, 8 dia. (top)

JOHN W. KRIEGSHAUSER
Kansas City, Mo.
Fern stand
Walnut
36 high; $150

WALTER S. BRYDE
Wilmington, Del.
Period secretary desk
Walnut
86 x 29-1/8 x 19-1/4

EJNER C. PAGH
Rockford, Ill.
Coffee table
Walnut
17 x 60

HOWARD WERNER
Deal Park, N.J.
Desk and chair set
Walnut, leather
29 x 48 x 36; $3,200

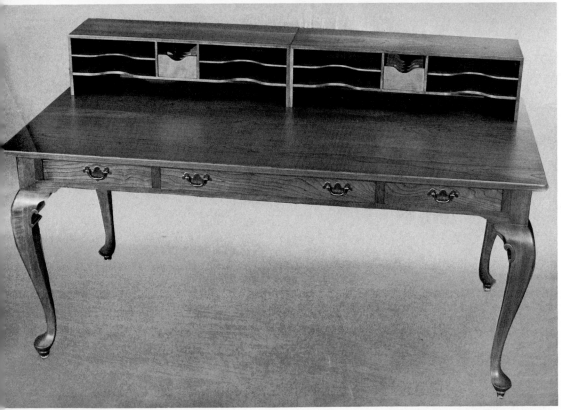

ALVIN WEAVER
Kansas City, Kans.
Queen Anne desk
Adirondack cherry
30 x 68-1/2 x 36

WALLACE H. HENDRY
Palo Alto, Calif.
Burl table
Redwood
19 high, 46 wide; $285

DOUG CHAPIN
Philadelphia, Pa.
Table
Walnut
29 high, 42 dia.

*"Base has turned pedestal; legs and
upper supports are hand carved."*

ROBERT C. WELCH
Erie, Colo.
Dining table
Oak
32 x 42 x 42; $375

*"Custom-made tiles by Garet Wohl
enable hot items and/or plants to be
set on table."*

MARTY SOBEL
Flemington, N.J.
Contemporary dining-room table
Walnut
76 x 40 x 29-1/2

MICHAEL COFFEY
Poultney, Vt.
''El Morro'' desk
Mozambique
37 x 68 x 36
Photo by Michael Aleshire

MARV PALLISCHECK
Fairport, N.Y.
Chopping-block table
Walnut, rock maple
36 x 36 x 20
Photo by Paul Wiedrich

 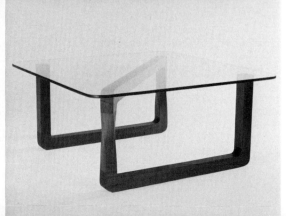

GEORGE W. BERRY
Rochester, N.Y.
Glass-top coffee table
Walnut
36 x 60 x 16-1/2; $1,150

JOHN NOEL
Mission, Kans.
Cocktail table
Teak, glass
30 x 30 x 14; $280

 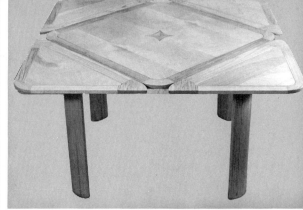

NORBERT MARKLIN
St. Louis, Mo.
Envelope-leaf table
Red oak, birch veneer
open: 28-3/4 x 55 square;
closed: 29-1/2 x 38-1/2 square

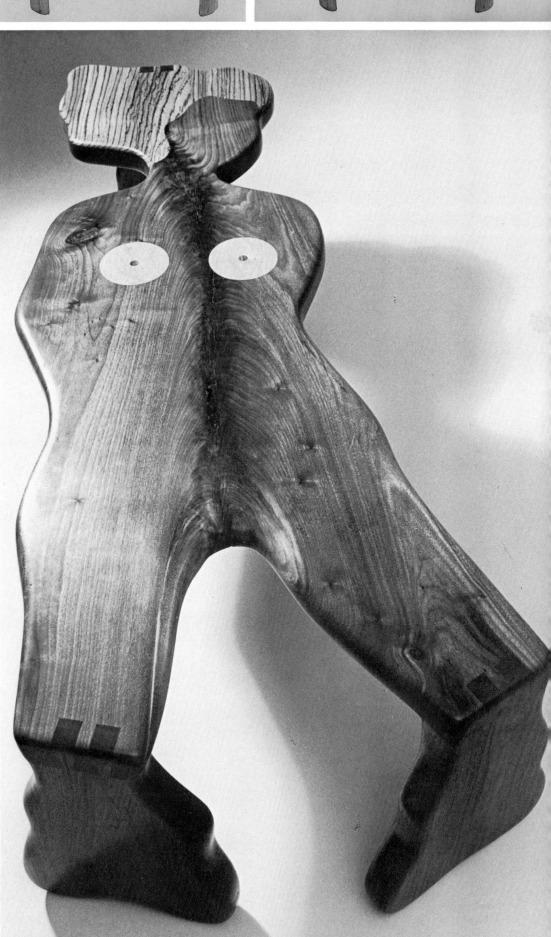

BOBBY R. FALWELL
De Kalb, Ill.
Lady table
Walnut, zebra, cherry
16 x 22 x 50

Beds, Benches and Couches

ARTHUR AHR (overleaf)
Sugar Loaf, N.Y.
Detail: cradle

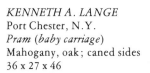

KENNETH A. LANGE
Port Chester, N.Y.
Pram (baby carriage)
Mahogany, oak; caned sides
36 x 27 x 46

ARTHUR AHR
Sugar Loaf, N.Y.
Cradle
Oak
$2,000
Photo by Robert E. Barrett

NOEL NORSKOG
Santa Fe, N. Mex.
Queen-size bed
Mahogany, with oak and rosewood
veneer
12 x 60 x 80; $1,200

*"The entire bed disassembles into 10
pieces without tools for easy moving."*

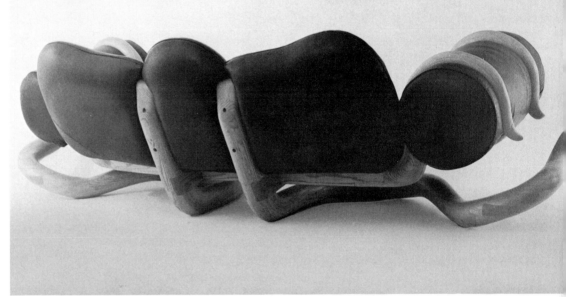

PETER DANKO
Alexandria, Va.
Sofa
Red oak, leather cushions
40 x 108; $5,500, plus cost of leather
or other fabric

*"Sofa is completely supported from
center of rear; no metal is used."*

J. CHRISTOPHER HECHT
Sagle, Idaho
Smiling bed
French, California and black walnut
60 x 66 x 87

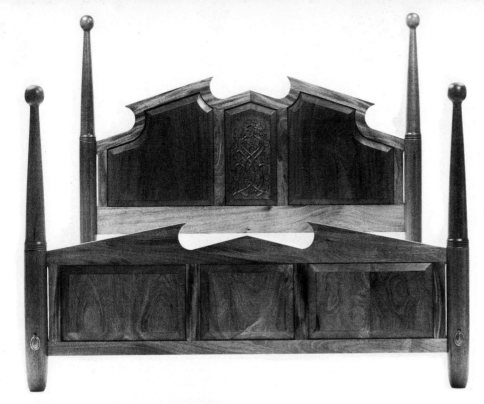

MICHAEL P. SHANKLIN
Newtonville, Mass.
Queen-size bed
Honduras mahogany
86 x 64 x 60; $1,600 (including
matching chest not shown here)

WALTER K. PRICE
Florence, Mass.
Queen-size bed
Cherry, black walnut
15 x 64 x 85
Photo by Robert Lyons

GEORGE H. RATHMELL
Los Osos, Calif.
Celure or partial (bed) canopy
Oak
68 x 36 x 144

*"Canopy has four panels of cut velvet
to relieve the all-wood feeling."*

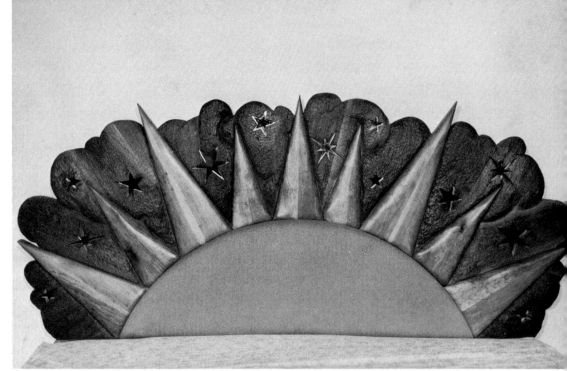

VICKI KASSOW
Southampton, Pa.
Headboard
Walnut, cherry, upholstered
centerpiece, mirrored stars
54 x 78

PHILIP O'LENO
Albion, Calif.
Queen-size bed
Redwood
54 x 66 x 89

*"I forge the candleholders in my
blacksmith shop."*

GLENN GORDON
Chicago, Ill.
Knock-down daybed and coffee table
Ash, steel
bed: 26 x 30 x 76
table: 15-1/2 x 20 x 48
Photo by Carole Harmel

JOZEF TARA & JOSEPH FEELY
Wiscasset, Maine
Bunk beds with dresser and storage
Birch
66 x 72 x 78

DON KENYON
Naples, N.Y.
Rocker with cradle
Pine, cherry, birch, maple, ash
38 x 20 x 49; $595

"...after the style of early mammy's benches."

FRANK KEYSER
Athens, N.Y.
Bench
White oak, ash
31-1/2 x 52-1/4

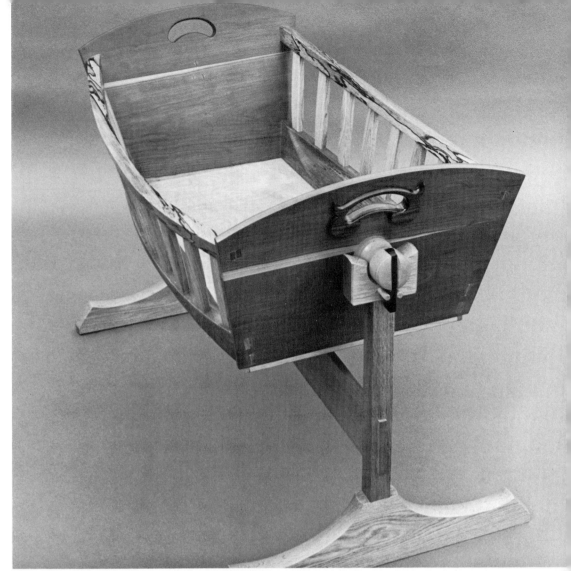

PETER LEAF
Oakland, Calif.
Cradle
Maple, cherry, oak, ebony, birch
$850

SIDNEY FLEISHER
Clarksville, N.Y.
Double bed
Cherry
16 x 60 x 79; headboard posts, 36 high
$195

*"The side rails slip into notches in the
footboard and headboard and are
bolted together with 3/8-in. carriage
bolts, one in each corner."*

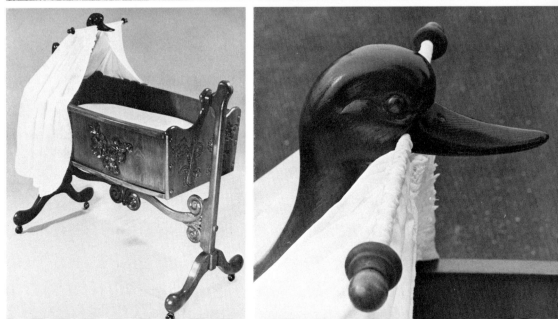

STEVEN A. HARTLEY
Orlando, Fla.
Cradle
Eastern white pine
41 x 20 x 42
*"...may be completely
disassembled for storage."*

Accessories

ANDY COOKLER (overleaf)
Boulder, Colo.
Detail: box
Zebrawood
3 x 9 x 5-1/2; $95

JUDI R. BARTHOLOMEW
Milwaukee, Wis.
Mulvaney nut bowl
Apple, gum
6 x 6 x 20; $400

ROGER SLOAN
Marcellus, Mich.
Twig pot
Walnut, inlaid with cross sections of
oak roots
3-1/4 high, 5 dia.; $35

ALEX DUNTON
Richmond, Va.
Three-legged carved bowl
10 x 7-1/2 x 3; $129

TOM MORTENSON
San Francisco, Calif.
Stave bowl
Koa, walnut
5-1/2 x 6; $75

DAVID BARCLAY
Rochester, N.Y.
Covered bowl
Walnut
7-1/4 high

JOZEF TARA & JOSEPH FEELY
Wiscasset, Maine
Stacking salad-bowl set
Cherry
16 high

MICHAEL HURWITZ
West Newton, Mass.
Turned bowl
Maple, walnut
9 dia.; $125

BOB TROTMAN
Casar, N.C.
Bowl
Cherry, walnut
12 wide

DENNIS F. RYAN
Rensselaer, N.Y.
Place setting
Zebrawood
dinner plates, 12-1/2 dia. ; $175 set

DEL STUBBS
Chico, Calif.
Dry-flower vases
Black walnut
10 high

MICHAEL ROCCANOVA
Bronx, N.Y.
Fruit/plant basket
Walnut, basswood
7 high, 7 dia. top

SAM BUSH
Pottstown, Pa.
Bowl
Birch burl
7 x 16 x 17; $1,500

STEPHEN HOGBIN
Caledon East, Ontario, Canada
Eggcup
Silky brown oak
4-1/3 high

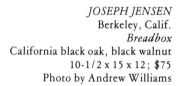

JOSEPH JENSEN
Berkeley, Calif.
Breadbox
California black oak, black walnut
10-1/2 x 15 x 12; $75
Photo by Andrew Williams

LON & DOTTIE MILLER
Fort Collins, Colo.
Step-stool
Walnut
18 x 15 x 16; $175

LEROY HOGUE
Spencerport, N.Y.
Mint dish, cracker dish
Walnut
mint dish: 2 x 4-1/2 x 8-1/4, $9
cracker dish: 1-5/8 x 2-1/2 x 24, $24
Photo by Stoney Point Studio

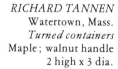

RICHARD TANNEN
Watertown, Mass.
Turned containers
Maple; walnut handle
2 high x 3 dia.

DONALD LLOYD McKINLEY
Mississauga, Ontario, Canada
Salad bowl
Black walnut (steam-bent)
5-1/2 x 20 x 13; $200

HAP SAKWA
Goleta, Calif.
Bud vase
California lilac
8 x 4; $24
Photo by Evans Stout

RUDE OSOLNIK
Berea, Ky.
Twig pots
larger: 7 high, 5 dia.; smaller: 2-1/2
high, 4-1/2 dia.

WILLIAM KRAVARIK
Brookfield Center, Conn.
Parquet teacup and saucer
Rosewood
cup: 2-1/2 high, 2-1/2 dia.; saucer:
1/2 high x 3-3/4 dia.

GALE E. KLOESEL
Austin, Tex.
Hardwood belt buckles
From top: laminate, rosewood,
cocobolo, rosewood, ebony
2-1/2 x 3-1/4; from $7 to $25

ALAN C. FOSTER
San Jose, Calif.
Belt buckles
Lacewood, rosewood, Honduras
rosewood, sycamore, tulipwood, black
locust, myrtle, rosewood, walnut
2-1/4 x 3-1/4; from $5 to $15

82

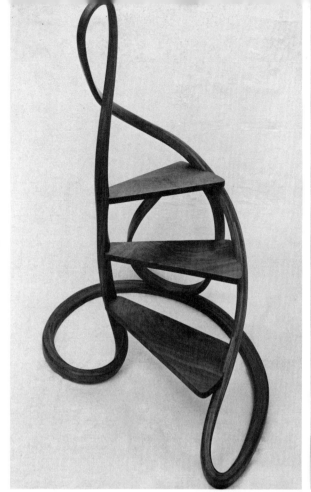

STEVEN A. FOLEY
Lake Oswego, Ore.
Mobius step
Black walnut (steam-bent)
51 x 36 x 24; $2,200

MAURY LETVEN
Philadelphia, Pa.
American Gothic foyer valet
Maple, stained glass, iron hardware
75 x 22 x 20; $900

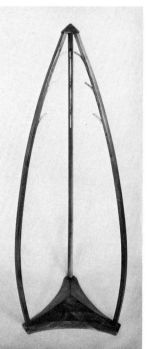

STEPHEN NUTTING
Gloucester, Mass.
Space closet
Black walnut, brass
70 x 24; $325
Photo by Mark Bernstein

KATHERINE A. SVEC
Tallahassee, Fla.
Four-section folding screen
Basswood
57 x 45 (unfolded)

KENNETH S. PHILLIPS
Fort Collins, Colo.
Vase
Rocky Mt. juniper
14 high

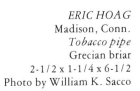

ERIC HOAG
Madison, Conn.
Tobacco pipe
Grecian briar
2-1/2 x 1-1/4 x 6-1/2
Photo by William K. Sacco

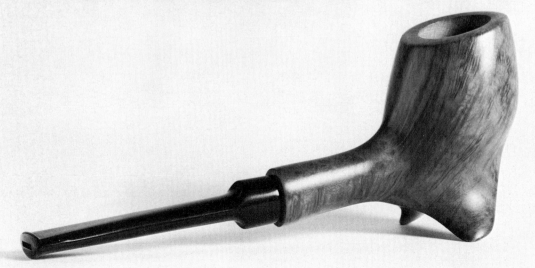

TIMOTHY McCLELLAN
Minneapolis, Minn.
Lidded box
Padauk, maple
4-1/2 x 12 x 8

STEPHEN K. LAUDERBACK
Bedford, Ind.
Oval sewing box
Walnut, rosewood
4-1/2 x 11-1/2 x 9-1/4
Photo by Roberts Studio

BRADLEY C. MILLER
Bangor, Pa.
Jewelry box
Chestnut, black walnut
3 x 8 x 11; $100

BOB BURT
Eugene, Ore.
Nesting and lined boxes
Various woods

84

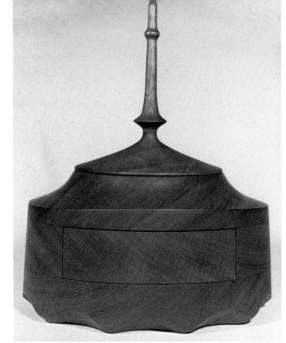

LEO G. DOYLE
San Bernardino, Calif.
Earring chest
Honduras mahogany
12 high; base, 10 x 8

"Mirror is on bottom of lid."

BRIAN DUNCAN
Great Falls, Mont.
Breadbox
Teak, oak, walnut, cherry, maple
14 x 18 x 12; $300
Photo by Donald Beans

*"The front is a tambour made and cut
from one piece of wood. Sliding out
from beneath the breadbox is a
cutting board."*

© *DAVID FLATT 1976*
Belleville, Wis.
Two-drawer chest
Cherry
6 x 8 x 3; $70

*"Drawers and case were cut
from single block."*

BILL LONG
St. Augustine, Fla.
Turned box
Partridgewood
9-1/2 dia.; $75

JOHN FOSSUM
Allston, Mass.
Jewelry box
Walnut, cherry
4 x 13 x 13; $300

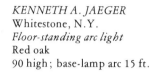

KENNETH A. JAEGER
Whitestone, N.Y.
Floor-standing arc light
Red oak
90 high; base-lamp arc 15 ft.

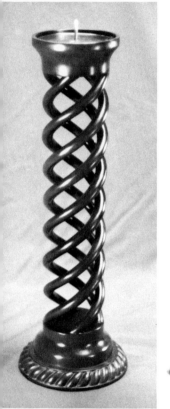

LEONARD BOSKEN
Cincinnati, Ohio
Candleholder
Cherry
15-3/4 high; base, 5-1/2 dia.

"...*turned from a 4 x 4 turning square, with an added piece for the base. The four 1/2-in. dia. spiral sides were then added by the use of a mortising chisel, router bit and hand-carving tools. The rope design was carved in the base.*"

HANS W. KOCH
Hanover, Pa.
Candleholder
Walnut
11 high; base, 5-1/2 dia.

MARTIN N. ALVEY
So. San Francisco, Calif.
Matched set of spiral candlesticks
Oak
11 high; base, 4 dia.

HOWARD C. OLDAKER
Glenwood, W. Va.
Lamp
Black walnut, cypress
16 x 7 dia. (center section)

DAVID GRINDAHL
San Bernardino, Calif.
Candlestick
Walnut
2-3/4 high, 5 dia.

"...*wood grain runs vertical for the candle cup and horizontal for the base.*"

PHIL CAMPBELL
Detroit, Mich.
Floor lamp
Walnut
60 high; $500

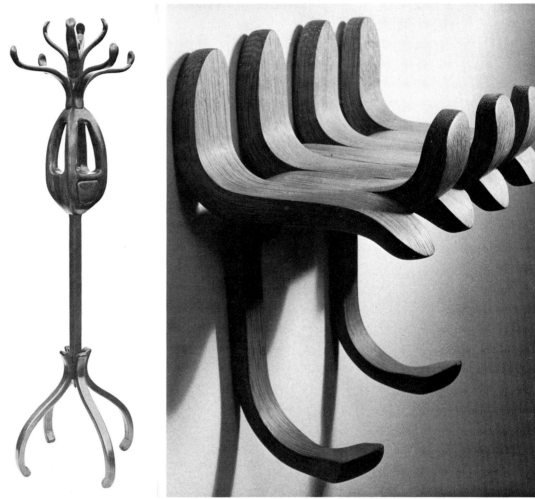

MARK LAWRENCE
Chico, Calif.
Clothes tree
Hawaiian koa
74 high; base, 24
Photo by R. K. Barney

RICHARD ESTEB
Lacey, Wash.
Coat / hat rack
White oak
11-1/2 x 11 x 7

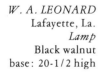

W. A. LEONARD
Lafayette, La.
Lamp
Black walnut
base: 20-1/2 high

*"The column of the base is made from
four pieces of 2 in. by 2 in. stock. The
four pieces are carved separately and
then assembled."*

JOHN R. HARVEY
Greenville, N.C.
Lamps X, XX
Walnut, cherry, blown glass
45 high

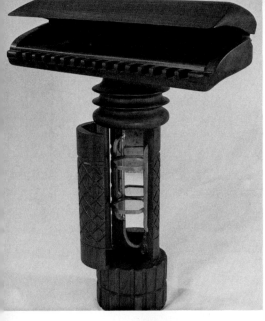

HUGH WESLER
Madison Wis.
Razor medicine chest
Walnut
25 x 18 x 8; $450

ARTHUR MEDORE, JR.
Hemet, Calif.
Jewelry cachet
Padauk
5 x 7 x 16; $110

STEVEN SPIRO
Appleton, Wis.
Clam boxes
Walnut, rosewood
dia: 4-1/2, 7-1/2, 10-1/2; $225

HAROLD E. HARDEN
Garberville, Calif.
Chest
Red oak, beech
7-7/8 x 10-5/8 x 6-5/8; $95

DENNIS F. RYAN
Rensselaer, N.Y.
Covered containers
Honduras rosewood, teak, bubinga
4 high

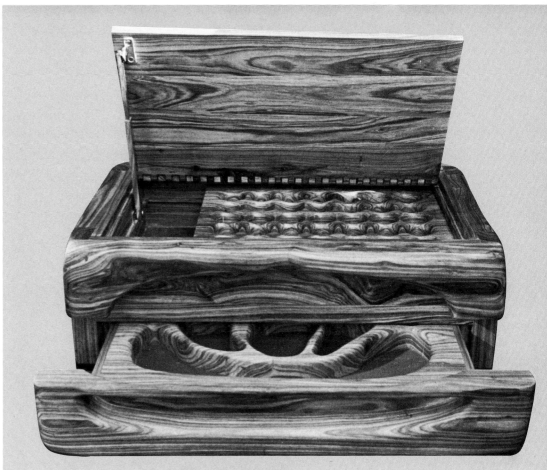

DAVID KROUSE
New York, N.Y.
Jewelry chest
Tulipwood
8 x 24 x 14

IRVING FISCHMAN
Cambridge, Mass.
Bowl (American Indian Series IV)
Teak, black walnut
4 high, 16 dia. ; $84

*"This is a reinterpretation of an
American Indian basketry concept into
wood. Laminated construction and
lathe turned."*

RICK VANDRUFF
Bellflower, Calif.
Jewelry box
Shedua
7 x 12 x 9

PHILIP NEREO
Windsor, Calif.
Small chest
Walnut, bay laurel, cherry
12 x 12 x 14 ; $400

DAVID TROE
Brighton, Mass.
Barrel of drawers
Walnut, ebony
18 long, 12 dia. ; $350

JOHN BICKEL
Ossining, N.Y.
Curio cabinet
Rosewood
24 x 16 x 12

"Sides, back and top are made as frames with mortise and tenon joints. Each frame was fabricated and assembled dry. Then the curved patterns were traced. They were reassembled with glue. After gluing, the curves were smoothed with spokeshave and files. The vacuum forming was done using each side, in turn, as a template for its own windows. A rectangular sheet of clear Uvex plastic was warmed to 350° F and placed over a frame arranged over a temporary plenum to which a shop vacuum was connected. After cooling the opening line was scribed and bandsawn 1/16-in. larger so it could be flexed and popped into its retaining slot."

TOM ECKERT
Tempe, Ariz.
Tambour container
Walnut
14 x 12 x 8

CRAIG S. DASCANIO
Brookline, Mass.
Small chest of drawers
Mahogany, satinwood
20 x 18 x 16

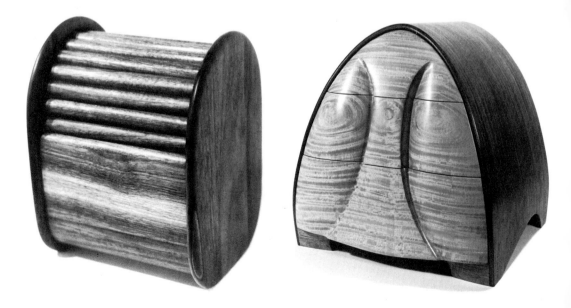

BOB KURZWEIL
GEORGE & MARGARET SHIPSTAD
Encino, Calif.
Art-supply box
Cherry
10-1/2 x 17-1/2 x 9
Photo by George Shipstad

RICHARD COHEN
Warwick, N.Y.
Bevel-topped box
Satinwood, mahogany, rosewood
4 x 7 x 11-1/8

IVAN KOCHAN
Oxford, Ohio
Jewelry box
Cedar
13 x 8 x 8; $450
Photo by George Hoxie

WILLIAM R. BROWN, JR.
Reisterstown, Md.
Bible box
Circasian walnut
9 x 15 x 6

''*The wood is salvaged from an old dresser and can be dated to about 1825. The box is lined with rose-colored velvet and is designed to hold the family Bible. The sides and top are carved with traditional relief and chip designs.*''

RICHARD E. PREISS
Scottsville, N.Y.
Jewelry chest
Andamon padauk, doussie, ebony
21-1/2 x 11-1/2 x 9-1/2

DOUGLAS R. HALEY
Butler, Ky.
Jewelry box
Black walnut
4-1/4 x 13 x 9; $500

"The top has an eleven-step wooden combination lock in it. The lock works by lining up the burl inlays on the protruding sticks with the edge of the top. There is only one order which includes eleven steps that will open and lock the box."

TERRY MILLER
Jaffrey, N.H.
Tool box
Mahogany, walnut
16 x 10 x 24

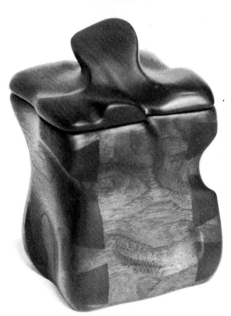

MITCHELL D. LANDY
Philadelphia, Pa.
Ring box
Walnut
9 dia.; $60

BOB TROTMAN
Casar, N.C.
Box
Walnut
7 x 3-1/2 x 3-1/2

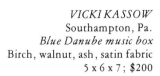

VICKI KASSOW
Southampton, Pa.
Blue Danube music box
Birch, walnut, ash, satin fabric
5 x 6 x 7; $200

MICHAEL S. CHINN
Long Beach, Calif.
Chest
Cherry, padauk, rosewood, birch
18 x 18 x 13

FRANCISCO PEREZ
South Meriden, Conn.
Jewelry box
Maple
5-1/2 x 10-1/4 x 8-3/4

ALFRED NEALE GORDON
Baton Rouge, La.
Music box
Plywood, maple burl veneer, walnut, rosewood
3-5/8 x 4-5/8 x 8-1/8

MARK LINDQUIST
Henniker, N.H.
Cloud box
Spalted maple
6 x 6 x 12; $250

94

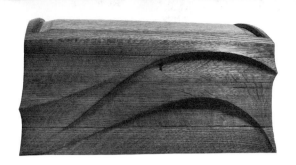

CHRISTOPHER MURRAY
Richmond, Va.
Silver chest
White oak
12 x 18 x 10; $200

"...*rift-sawn, lined with Pacific
silver-cloth, a tarnish preventative.*"

AMIL ST. AUGUSTINE
Novato, Calif.
Jewelry box
Cherry, ironwood
8-1/2 x 16 x 25; $600

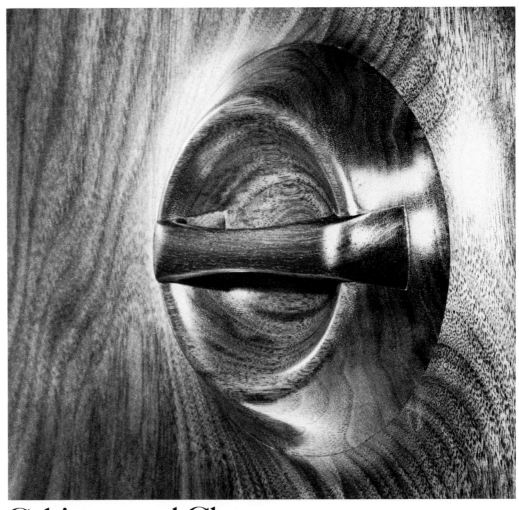

Cabinets and Chests

NEIL WEHRLIE (overleaf)
El Cerrito, Calif.
Detail: file cabinet

JOHN E. CARLSON
Lawndale, Calif.
Bureau
Pine; mahogany and rosewood
veneer; maple veining
31-1/2 x 39 x 21; $2,000
Photo by Hedman's Photo Studio

"*. . .in the Swedish rococo style.*"

TOM MORTENSON &
KEVIN MAHER
San Francisco, Calif.
Hutch bookcase
Koa
78 x 48; $1,200

VINCENT P. LINDER
Atlantic Mine, Mich.
China cupboard
Yellow birch, walnut veneer
72 x 40 x 16

*"The top of the bottom section
includes a slide-out center piece with a
concealed slate top for hot dishes. The
top section includes an inside
cabinet light."*

JOHN PETERSON
Brookline, Mass.
Wall cabinet
Walnut
33 x 16-1/4 x 8-1/2; $625

HOWARD KAVINSKY
Chicago, Ill.
Liquor cabinet
Cherry
72 x 17 x 10; $450

CURTIS MINIER
Seattle, Wash.
Horizontal file cabinet
Koa, oak
29 x 20 x 50; $450
Photo by Joan Sisson

E. E. ''SKIP'' BENSON
San Francisco, Calif.
Music stand and storage unit
Cherry
32 x 16 x 24

''...made specifically for a violin.
Drawer becomes a music stand.''

BILL KORRELL
Erie, Pa.
Night stand/suspended cabinet
Black walnut
25-1/2 high; cabinet, 20 x 12

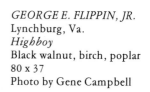

GEORGE E. FLIPPIN, JR.
Lynchburg, Va.
Highboy
Black walnut, birch, poplar
80 x 37
Photo by Gene Campbell

MITCHELL AZOFF
Avon, N.Y.
Liquor cabinet
Oak, elm
29 x 42 x 17

JOE HOGAN
Lynn, Mass.
Dry-sink hutch
White pine
85 x 72; $2,300

THOM HUCKER
Brookline, Mass.
Split cabinet
Walnut, solid and veneer
44 x 60 x 22; $1,800

*"The majority of the solid joints are
traditional triple-miter Chinese joints.
There is a space between frame and
panel. I wanted that play of space in
the piece—it was a major theme—just
as the two parts of the piece are
separate units, suspended by hidden
laminates underneath."*

WESLEY BRETT
Grand Island, N.Y.
Collector's item number two
Teak
Photo by Michael Myers

"*A cabinet for the storage and display of a collection of guide fossils. At the base of the cabinet a drawer for 3 x 5 file catalog is provided with a compartment for magnifying glasses, picks, etc. Rotating bins are splined miter boxes suspended on a steel shaft using twelve bearings of the type used for back-up wheels on many band saws.*"

JOHN M. MONTGOMERY
Victoria, B.C., Canada
Revolving book case
Satin walnut, imbuya
31-1/2 x 20 x 20
Photo by Ian McKain

"*This provides six feet of shelving plus a dictionary stand.*"

104

ACORN WOODWORKS
Tuscon, Ariz.
Jewelry box
Walnut
52 x 16 x 18
Photo by Tim Fuller

STEVEN VOORHEIS
Missoula, Mont.
Linen cabinet
Mahogany
34 x 22 x 9; $720

PAUL J. WEDEL II
Leola, Pa.
Wall-hung liquor cabinet
Black walnut, bird's-eye maple
22 x 27 x 7

DEAN TORGES & JACK GUTILLA
Ostrander, Ohio
Corner cabinet
Curly and bird's-eye maple
79-3/4 high, 40-3/8 wide; $2,900

MICHAEL COFFEY
Poultney, Vt.
Ovation
Butternut, birch
80 x 47 x 29; $4,020

"Laminated doors wrap around triangular-shaped stereo cabinet that hangs in a corner."

PETER GOLLUP
Waynesville, N.C.
Blanket chest
White oak
22 x 18 x 30
Photo by Wendy Holmes

106

KINGSLEY C. BROOKS
Cambridge, Mass.
Cabinet
Walnut, crotch walnut veneer
30 x 30 x 20; $500

CARL A. ZANONI
Middletown, Conn.
Display cabinet
Veneers, walnut, ebony, gumwood
73 x 42 x 15
Photo by David A. Thorstensen

*"The asymmetrical cantilevered plank
and the asymmetrical shelves serve as a
counterpoint to the bold symmetry of
the Rorschach-pattern doors."*

WILLIAM D. CHERKIN
Rochester, N.Y.
Box turtle toy chest
Oak, walnut
16 x 18 x 36

JOHN W. KRIEGSHAUSER
Kansas City, Mo.
Buffet cabinet
Mahogany
32 x 48; $450

PAUL CUSACK
Philadelphia, Pa.
Blanket chest
Maple
28 x 20 x 48; $1,500

BRUCE BEEKEN
Allston, Mass.
Wall-hung cabinet
Maple
28 x 19 x 12

EDGAR ANDERSON
Morristown, N.J.
Jewelry chest
Black walnut
33 x 32 x 20
pedestal, 24 high; $4,000

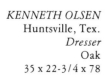

JOHN DUNNIGAN
Saunderstown, R.I.
Wall cabinet
Teak, beech
22 x 14 x 6; $200

KENNETH OLSEN
Huntsville, Tex.
Dresser
Oak
35 x 22-3/4 x 78

*"Front and side angle is 7 degrees.
Behind the doors are four drawers."*

109

ROBERT BALDWIN
Corvallis, Ore.
Hutch
White oak, black walnut
88 x 52 x 20

JON O. GRONDAHL
Staten Island, N.Y.
Hope chest
Mahogany, birch
20 x 18 x 36

Chest of drawers
Pine
42 x 26 x 18

''Both pieces hand-painted in oil
colors, in Norwegian rosepainting
style. 'Bestefars Jente' is Norwegian for
'grandfather's girl.' ''

FRANK J. BECHT
Buffalo, N.Y.
Hall mirror
Red oak
40 x 22 x 11; $128

MICHAEL CIARDELLI
Milford, N.H.
Wall-hung storage cabinet
Mahogany
30 x 12 x 8

SASWATHAN QUINN
San Francisco, Calif.
Lawyer's bookshelf
Shedua
119 x 98

STEVE HILL
Scottsville, N.Y.
Blanket chest
Maple, cherry, honey locust
16 x 20 x 34

LEW KORN
Larchmont, N.Y.
Blanket chest
Curly maple, walnut
27 x 42 x 20; $950
Photo by Bob Zucker

ROBERT M. SOULE
West Haven, Conn.
Music cabinet
Cherry
33 x 18-1/2 x 72

"The unit has the following features:
record player, record storage, pre-amp
and tuner, record player for 78 rpm
records, drawers for tape storage,
speaker controls, and tape deck."

RICHARD ROBERGE
Providence, R.I.
Wall cabinet
Rosewood, ebony
23 x 9 x 5-1/2; $350

WENDY L. MARUYAMA
Newton, Mass.
Blanket chest
Walnut, ebony
20 x 18 x 34

RON DEKOK
Belleville, Wis.
Compartmental chest
Mahogany and oak ply
36 dia.; $1,500

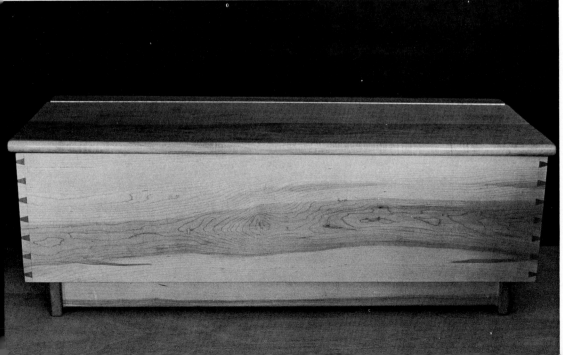

ROBERT BEISWINGER
Millstone, N.J.
Chest
Sugar maple
17-1/4 x 21 x 50

"Height allows use as a bench."

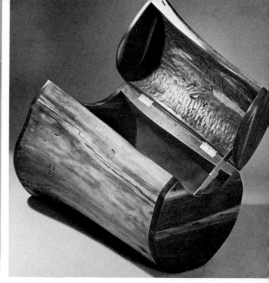

BOBBY R. FALWELL
De Kalb, Ill.
Log chest
Walnut
24-1/2 x 26 x 30

ROBERT W. BAILEY
Woodleaf, N.C.
Chest on chest
Cherry, cedar
58 x 33 x 19

RICHARD LaBOSSIERE
Towaco, N.J.
Secretary bookcase
African mahogany
88-1/2 x 64

ROBERT DONOVAN
Worcester, Mass.
Sea chest
Walnut, birch, calfskin, brass
18 x 39 x 20; $900

TAGE FRID
Foster, R.I.
Sideboard
Walnut
36 x 60 x 18

NEIL WEHRLIE
El Cerrito, Calif.
File cabinet
Walnut, oak, rosewood
$1,400

"The drawer front is laminated, turned and sculpted, then inset with a dovetailed rosewood handle."

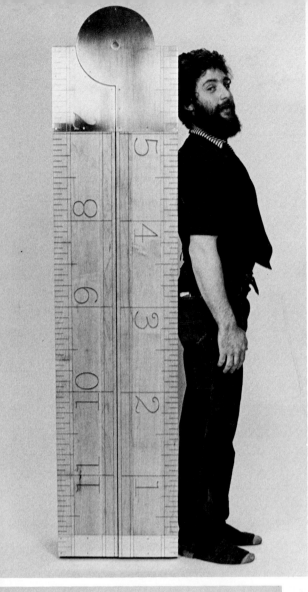

LEROY SCHUETTE
Durham, N.H.
Boxwood rule cabinet
Maple, brass
78 x 10 x 18; $5,000

PATRICK ROBBINS
Pontiac, Mich.
Portrait of Carol; self-portrait
Carol, walnut; Patrick, mahogany
Carol: 54 x 9 x 12; $500
Patrick: 58 x 9 x 14

"The inspiration for these two pieces is the figure. The height, width, location of shelves, etc. come directly from specifically measured figures (myself and my wife). I have simplified the figure into basic geometric shapes. The hinges and latches are hidden from view so that the viewer must explore the piece to discover how to open the various compartments."

CHRIS BECKSVOORT
New Gloucester, Maine
Cupboard
Red oak
75 x 24 x 17; $620

WILLIAM BROOKS &
PETER MAYNARD
Alstead, N.H.
Blanket chest
Cherry, cedar
22 x 44 x 22; $600

STEPHEN B. CRUMP
Memphis, Tenn.
Secretary
Pecan
74 x 44 x 24

© *JOHN STANLEY*
Middleboro, Mass.
Sandi Z blanket chest
Maple, ash, pine
42 x 36 x 26

Carving, Sculpture and Marquetry

MORSE CLARY (overleaf)
Pasco, Wash.
Detail: Vanishing specie

MICHAEL M. POLLAK
Syracuse, N.Y.
Involuted cube
Mahogany
8 x 8 x 8

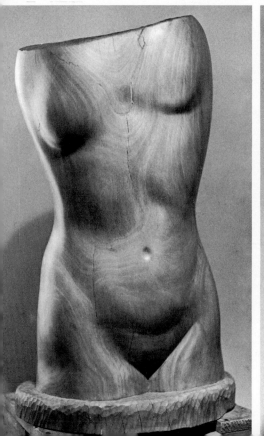

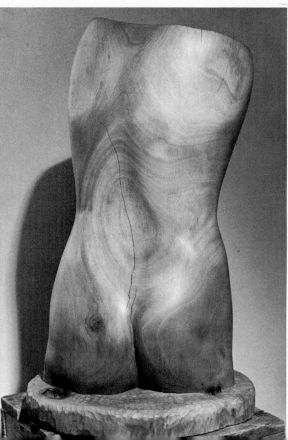

GALE A. JAMIESON
Baltimore, Md.
Torso study
Sycamore
22 high

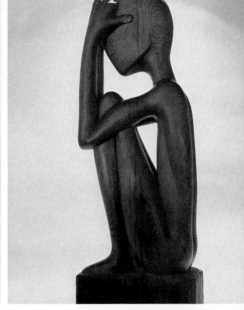

ALBERT WEISMAN
Wakefield, Mass.
Girl, kneeling
Elm
10 high; $300

JOEL GOTTLIEB
Glen Cove, N.Y.
Hiatus
Pine
34 x 7 x 12

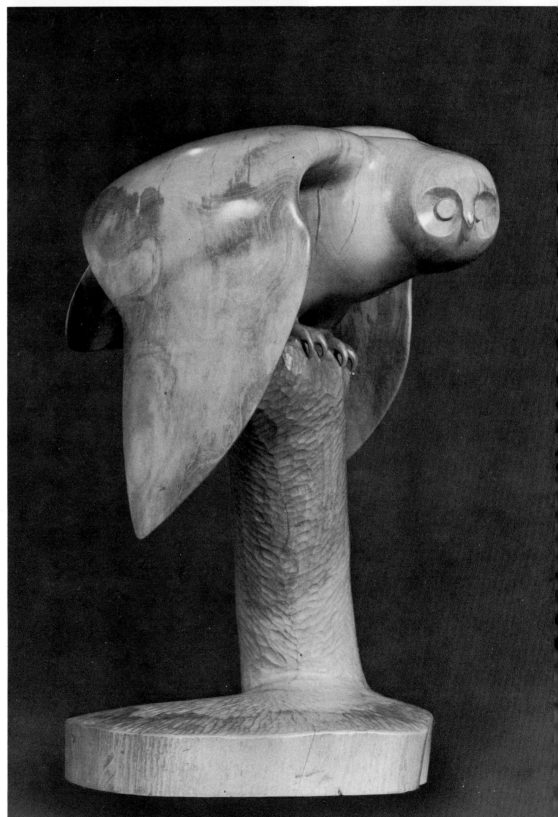

ORREN HUTTER
Northridge, Calif.
Stylized owl
Oraige
20 high x 13 wide; $1,200

123

AGNES LILGE
Altadena, Calif.
Merrymaker
Maple
13-1/2 x 7 x 9-1/2

JUDITH BRINOVEC
Port Washington, Wis.
Sunny
Basswood
4 x 4 x 9-1/2; $90

LOWELL D. BINGHAM
Merced, Calif.
Leprechaun
Basswood
8-1/2 high

DON M. HILL
Trout Creek, Mont.
Old cowboy
23 different woods

WARD MILLER, JR.
Sycamore, Ill.
The lighthouse keeper
Basswood (painted)
10 x 4 x 6; $300

IGOR GIVOTOVSKY
Amesbury, Mass.
The jazzman
Zebra, tulip, spalted English yew,
poplar
9-1/2 x 11-1/4 x 4

JOHN M. MOSTY
Kerrville, Tex.
Sunset ride
Satinwood, French walnut,
black walnut
10 x 25

HANS PETER LANGER
Forest, Va.
Grist mill
Mahogany
12-1/2 x 18

JAMES W. MARTIN
Montvale, N.J.
Space doll
Paldoa, narra, avodire, birch,
gumwood, padauk, holly,
oriental wood
34 x 21

ROSALIE SHERMAN
Gulph Mills, Pa.
The dance
Mahogany, poplar
66 x 42 x 24

125

DEL DISHER
Bethany, Conn.
Flames in walnut
Walnut
12 x 11 x 2

MORSE CLARY
Pasco, Wash.
Germination
Red willow
32 x 20 x 25; $900

*"...designed around removal of center
core to avoid excessive checking."*

ROBERT FREEMAN
Newton Center, Mass.
Ball in cage
Maple, yellow birch

JO-AN SMITH
Las Cruces, N. Mex.
Jewelry holder
Brazilian rosewood

IGOR GIVOTOVSKY
Amesbury, Mass.
*The elms: silent witnesses of our past
keep their secrets*
Mahogany, walnut, elm
32 x 24 x 19-1/2

126

JOSEPH S. WHEELWRIGHT
Cambridge, Mass.
Earthman
Birch, ash, mahogany, pine
75 high; $2,200

MARK JACKSON
Dearborn Heights, Mich.
Double-pierced form
Walnut
24 high; $800

JERRY LERNER
Park Forest, Ill.
Quartic translation
Honduras mahogany
16 x 8 x 8

*"This abstract geometrical sculpture
is a mathematical surface represented
by a quartic equation. The horizontal
ridge extending around the sculpture
halfway up lies in the x-y plane."*

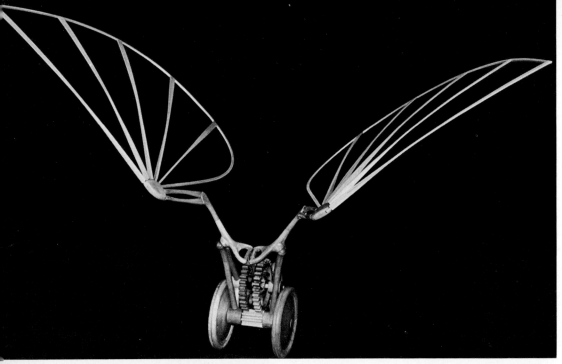

PHILIP PIEPER
Dennis, Mass.
Flying machine
Birch, maple
84 wingspan; $2,000

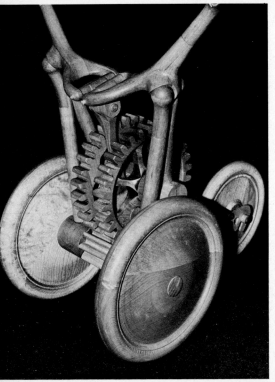

DAVID C. ROY
South Woodstock, Conn.
Serendipity
Baltic birch plywood
10 x 20 x 4; $150

"...*kinetic wall sculpture, with
weight-driven clock-like escapement
mechanism constructed entirely of
wood. The upper wheel rolls in a track
along the top of the sculpture. It is
kept in motion through the action of
the weight-driven gear and ratchet
mechanism. The weight is suspended
below the sculpture by a system of
strings and pulleys. It is raised by
turning the ratchet gear clock-wise.
Serendipity will stay in motion for
about 35 minutes on a single
winding.*"

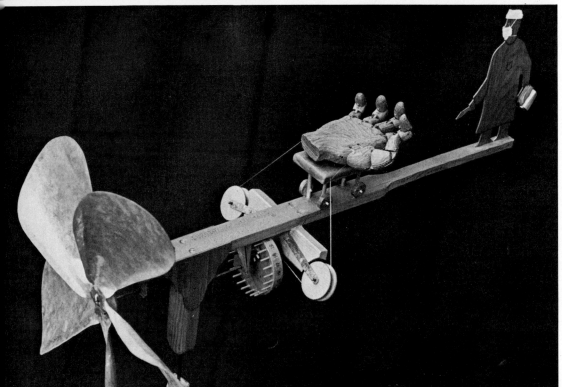

WILLIAM F. KEYSER
Arlington, Va.
"Surgery of the hand" wind machine
Pine, birch-veneer plywood, sheet
metal
36 long

"*The hand is normal adult size. The
piece is mounted and swivels on the
metal shaft directly behind the
propeller. The man (surgeon) acts as a
vane to turn the piece into the wind.
The propeller turns reduction gears.
Off-center pin on large gear pulls fish
line tendons which open and close the
hand. The hand contains all finger and
thumb joints. The machine operates
very smoothly in a light wind. The
hand moves frantically in a heavy
wind. This whirligig was made as a
tradesman's shingle for my brother
who is a hand surgeon.*"

JOSEPH S. WHEELWRIGHT
Cambridge, Mass.
Dancers and dreamers
Walnut, padauk, maple, butternut,
ebony, birch
37 x 21

CATHY MAYER COHEN
Riverside, Calif.
Bracelet
Ebony, purpleheart, ivory, silver

*"The wood and silver were laminated
together, then carved and sanded."*

EDWARD J. BARRY
La Grange Highlands, Ill.
Implosion
White pine
8 x 8 x 5/8; $75

RICHARD R. BREITENBACH
Baltimore, Md.
Rocking form
Ash, cherry
72 x 48 x 96; $1,800

*"...done by modular offset
lamination technique."*

RALPH K. EVANS
Chatsworth, Calif.
Full-scale tool replicas
Clamp: rosewood, maple; level:
walnut, lemon; square: ebony,
goncalo alves, maple

CHARLES E. McELREA
Long Beach, Calif.
Neuschwanstein castle, Bavaria
Avodire, poplar burl, myrtle burl,
vermilion, harewood
22 x 28; $3,000

ALBERT C. PARKER
Old Greenwich, Conn.
Evening watch
18-1/2 x 13-1/2

WILLIAM MacCREA
Alfred Station, N.Y.
Dove panel
Rosewood, black walnut, cherry gum,
sumac
25 x 36
Photo by William G. Moogan

*"...one of a three-piece set. Each
panel symbolizes one part of the
Trinity and is full
of religious symbols."*

HERSCHEL E. WESTBROOK
Columbus, Ohio
Sunny afternoon (hanging mural)
Walnut
24 x 27-1/8 x 2-3/8 overall; $1,150

HARRY R. TYLER, JR.
Wiscasset, Maine
Killdeer in flight
Bubinga

RICHARD O. PROBST
Indianapolis, Ind.
Untitled
Walnut
21 x 11-1/2 x 1-1/2

RITA DUNIPACE
Brookline, Mass.
Lizards
Maple
2 x 7-1/2 x 17; $400

HARRY HITCHNER
Hollandale, Wis.
Sharecropper's wife
Cherry
61 high; $1,800

R. BRUCE HOADLEY
Amherst, Mass.
Captive: Who?
Catalpa
11-1/2 high
Photo by Russell Mariz

". . . carved from a single block of wood. Figures are interlocked but stand separately without touching."

132

JAMES SANDBERG
Albion, Calif.
Falcon in hand
Madrone driftwood
14 high
Photos by Judith Brown

STAN NIBLACK
Upland, Calif.
Madonna foreshadowed
American walnut
38 x 4 x 6; shadow length, 36

JANE JASKEVICH
Tallahassee, Fla.
Struggle
Fir
36 x 4; $350

JOHN ROCUS
Ann Arbor, Mich.
Mountain music
Black walnut
23-2/5 high; $200

JORDAN IVANOV
Philadelphia, Pa.
Swimmer
Elm
18 x 36; $5,000

REX P. VAUGHT
Fremont, Calif.
Football
Hinds, black walnut, African
mahogany, bird's-eye maple
11-1/8 long, 6-11/16 dia.; $335

JOSEPH L. KANIG
Wings of fancy
Holly, avodire, pear, butternut,
lacewood, benin, sapele, narra,
rosewood
19-1/2 x 19-1/2

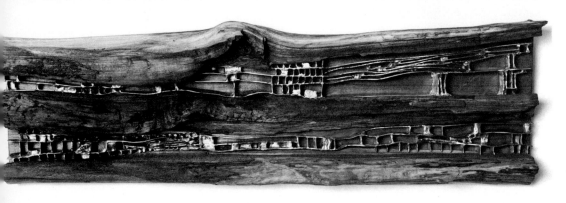

JOHN LEVERING
Columbia, Md.
Strata
Walnut
38 long; $650

MITCH KILGORE
Franklington, La.
Sign: open and closed
Cypress, white oak, birch
16-1/2 x 25-1/2 x 2-1/2

WENDY HYDE
Providence, R.I.
Table
Philippine mahogany; veneers:
fiddleback mahogany, ash, rosewood,
zebrawood, walnut, curly maple, tiger
maple, mahogany, teak
17 high x 24 dia.

*"Marquetry design includes Canada
geese, mallards, pintails and seagulls."*

134

DOOLAEGE & MACBRIDE
FURNITUREMAKERS
Oakland, Calif.
Boxes
Redwood
7 x 11-3/4 x 20-1/2
squid, $250; willow, $230
Photos by John Hyde

ED ROBINS
Cape Town, South Africa
De Boekenwurm
24 x 36

WILLIAM BREWERTON
Canandaigua, N.Y.
Pacific sunset
Rosa perobo, rosewood,
walnut, mahogany
8 x 10

RON & HELEN VELLUCCI
Houston, Tex.
Renaissance maiden
Oak, purple heart, mahogany, birch,
padauk, ash, parana pine, white pine,
bird's-eye maple, poplar, walnut,
plywood
77-1/8 x 45; $8,000

MARK SMITH
New Meadows, Idaho
Dinnerware
Black walnut
Photo by Ed Caraeff

"The dinnerware represented here is
part of a six-plate service. Each dinner
plate is carved from a solid block, and
the life forms are life-sized. The theme
of the set is Southern California coastal
life. Each animal is associated with
flora it would likely be found with,
such as the iguanas with prickly pear
cactus and the pond turtle and beetle
with oak leaves. The pieces are
functional as well as decorative."

ROBERT K. SEARLES
Union Center, Wis.
"To Know the Clouds"
Canada Geese
Basswood
Wingspread of upper bird, 18

*"Every wing and body feather is carved
separately (over 4,000 individual
pieces) and applied to solid blocks
carved to shape. Only the middle toe
of the upper bird touches the second
primary of the lower bird."*

DON BRIDDELL
Dallastown, Pa.
Drake and hen mallard
Balsa, pine
each 14 x 8 x 6

Instruments and Tools

MARK RUDDY (overleaf)
Duluth, Minn.
Detail: spinning wheel

CHRISTOPHER F. BANNISTER
Hopewell, N.J.
Grand piano
**Cypress, rosewood, ebony, holly,
amboyne burl; $42,000**

JOHN PIERSON
Pacific Beach, Calif.
Music stand for violist
White oak, fiddleback mahogany,
ebony
73-1/2 high; $750

R. E. BUSHNELL
Sturbridge, Mass.
*Philadelphia Chippendale
tall-case clock*
Mahogany, butternut, white pine
90-5/8 x 24-3/16 x 11-7/16

WALTER G. TOROSIAN
Fresno, Calif.
Display cabinet and clock
Black walnut, glass, bronze
68 x 15 x 15
Photo by Crystal Photography

*"The light units are circles of 1-1/2-in.
neon tubing. One is located in the
clock-face cube and the other in the
base cube. Each tube has a transformer
and both are supported in a walnut
and Plexiglas cradle. To conceal the
electric wiring in the walls, a groove
was routed out, zigzagging from one
side to the other because of the open
ends. The clock mechanism is battery
operated and located just above the
top neon tube. The letters of the
hour-designations were cast in lead and
then gold leafed. Applying pressure
for gluing was a problem because of
the open sides. Consequently, every
piece of wood was hand glued
separately and assembled as one unit
because of the change in direction of
the grain pattern from
horizontal to vertical."*

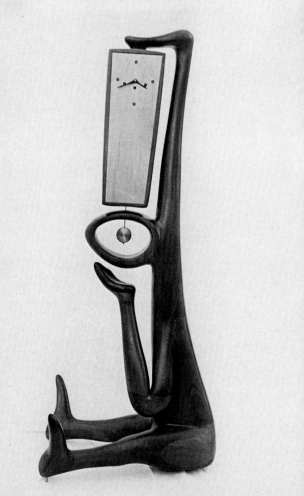

THOMAS A. SANDBERG
Galesburg, Ill.
Grandmother clock
Cherry, smoked Plexiglas
63 x 15 x 10

ETHAN PERRY
Erwinna, Pa.
Time on my hands
Mahogany
74 high

141

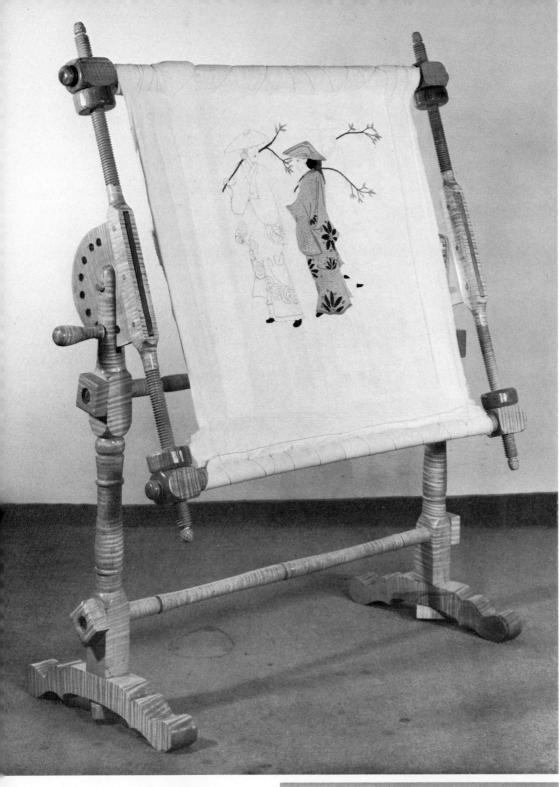

THOMAS J. DUFFY &
JOSEPH McDONALD
Ogdensburg, N.Y.
Needlepoint frame
Curly maple
36 high, 33 wide;
Photo by Allen Photography

MARVIN PECK, JR.
Albany, Ga.
Grandfather clock
Walnut
80 x 18-1/2 x 13

T. C. GRAVES
Knoxville, Tenn.
Clock
Cherry
13 x 11 x 5-1/2; $259
Photo by Ron Warwick Studio

ARVLE E. MARSHALL
Athens, Ga.
Spinning wheel
Red oak, maple
great wheel, 28 dia.
bench 8 x 24 x 1-1/2 ; $350

*". . . of traditional design but with
modern modifications:
counterbalanced great wheel, ball
bearings, large spinning orifice and
large bobbin to allow the spinner to
create the special and thick yarns with a
smooth-running balanced wheel."*

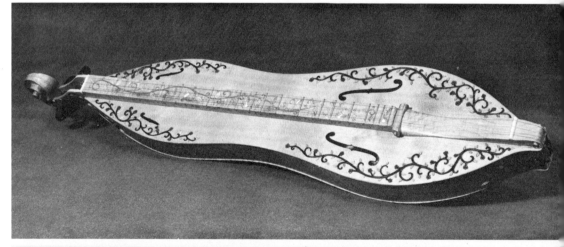

BOB TOOL
Chesterfield, N.J.
Dulcimer
Bird's-eye maple, spruce, black
walnut, cherry, birch
32-1/2 x 7-1/4 x 2-1/2
Photo by Joseph McBride

JOHN POMEROY &
CORY COLBURN
Vernonia, Ore.
Music stand
Black walnut
64 high

CHESTER KNIGHT
Houston, Tex.
Foot-treadle lathe
Ash
37 x 40 x 25

"The only metal is in the flywheel
shaft, head spindle and tail stock
screw. The treadle is cut out to reduce
weight, not as decoration. In fact, I
tried to keep the design as austere as
possible. The lathe can be
disassembled entirely by withdrawing
the tusk tenon wedges."

CHARLES M. RUGGLES
Cleveland, Ohio
House organ
Fumed white oak
77 x 30 x 58-1/2; $10,000

LEROY SCHUETTE
Durham, N.H.
Surface gauge music stand
Cherry
63 high

BART BRUSH
Cherry Valley, N.Y.
Hurdy-gurdy
Walnut
24 long; $400

JOHN D. ALEXANDER, JR.
Baltimore, Md.
Tape loom
Cherry
36 high, 32 long

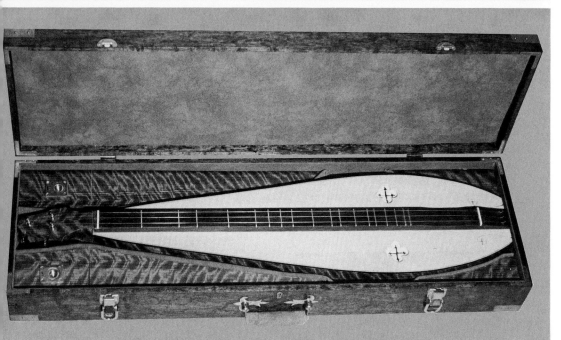

TOM MUSCO
Orange, Mass.
Appalachian dulcimer and case
Waco wood, rosewood, spruce,
mahogany
dulcimer, 35 x 8 x 2-1/2
case, 36-1/2 x 11 x 5

ROBSON SPLANE, JR.
Northridge, Calif.
Treadle jigsaw
Oak, rosewood
47-1/2 x 34 x 23-1/2; throat, 14

PHILLIP J. PETILLO
Ocean, N.J.
Steel-string guitar
Rosewood, spruce, curly maple, ebony
41-1/4 x 15-1/4 x 4-7/8; $2,800
Photo by Page Photo Service

WALTER HOLTKAMP, designer
FRED BRAUCKSIEK, maker
Cleveland, Ohio
Portable pipe organ
Cherry, ebony, boxwood

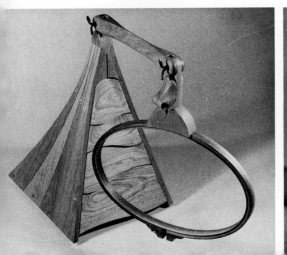

LAURENCE HENDRICKS
New Preston, Conn.
Embroidery hoop/cabinet
Cherry, walnut
24 high; hoop, 12 x 18

MARK RUDDY
Duluth, Minn.
Spinning wheel
Yellow birch
32 high, 35 long

STEPHEN B. RINGLE
Somerville, Mass.
Adjustable quilting frame
Cherry, redwood
32-5/8 x 51 to 87 x 31-1/2

*"The work is attached to the poles
with thumbtacks and rolled from one
pole to the other as the quilting
progresses. Shown in its fully extended
position for a queen-size quilt, the
frame may be shortened by loosening
the four brass wing nuts on the lower
stretchers and repositioning the pegs
in the poles, which are drilled at 3-in.
intervals from one end. The frame is
easily dismantled when not in use."*

PETER SUPERTY
Sunderland, Mass.
Concave plane
Maple, rosewood
13 x 2-1/4 x 3-1/2
Photo by David Stansbury

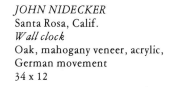

JOHN NIDECKER
Santa Rosa, Calif.
Wall clock
Oak, mahogany veneer, acrylic,
German movement
34 x 12

*"The design is an attempt to move
away from traditional approaches and
be conservatively modern. The use of
Roman numerals and scroll hands
provides a tie with the past and
contrasts with the simple lines of the
case."*

HAROLD E. CARTY
Piney Flats, Tenn.
Table clock
Wormy chestnut, walnut, triple-chime
movement
21-1/4 x 14-1/2 x 8-7/8; $350

ALVAN HILL
Ashford, Conn.
Set of planes
Maple
9-1/4 x 3-3/8; width varies

*"The iron seats at 50°. Steel is tool,
5/16 in. thick."*

EDUARDO A. RUMAYOR
Bronx, N.Y.
Dado saw
Brazilian imbuya
13-1/4 x 9 x 1-1/16

Kebiki
Mansonia, ebony, crabapple
8 x 8-3/4 x 2-3/4

*". . . a traditional Japanese cutting
gauge, designed to cut or slice up to
3/4-in. clear softwood stock."*

JOHN POMEROY &
CORY COLBURN
Vernonia, Ore.
Cider press
Oak, walnut, rosewood, brass
stainless steel
45 x 30 x 47; $1,500

*"With this press, thirty gallons of cider
were easily pressed in an afternoon."*

151

JOHN & SCOTT CURRIER
Northwood, N.H.
Jack loom (detail below)
Maple, black walnut
41-1/2 x 56 x 35-1/2; $590

STEPHEN K. LAUDERBACK
Bedford, Ind.
Embroidery stand
Walnut
26 to 34 high (adjustable); work
surface, 12; $150

"*The function of the stand is to hold
needlework at chair height. The hoop
height is adjusted by the side knob.
The top knob adjusts the rotation of
the hoop, so that work can be turned
180° to work on the back of a piece.
The smaller knob in the front adjusts
the tension of the outer hoop, so that
work can be inserted and removed,
allowing for various thicknesses of
material.*"

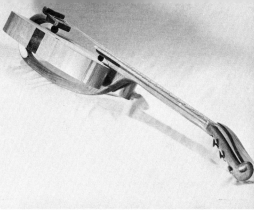

STEVEN A. HARTLEY
Orlando, Fla.
Guitar
Walnut, mahogany, teak,
birch, spruce
38 x 14 x 6-1/2

"*...designed to produce
sound through vibration of the entire
frame transferrred to the sound box by
an adjustable post on the underside.
This device provides variable
tone and volume.*"

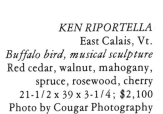

KEN RIPORTELLA
East Calais, Vt.
Buffalo bird, musical sculpture
Red cedar, walnut, mahogany,
spruce, rosewood, cherry
21-1/2 x 39 x 3-1/4; $2,100
Photo by Cougar Photography

"*The clients requested two separate
fingerboards to be played by the
husband and wife, facing each other.
There are two separate sound chambers
designed to produce sympathetic tone
qualities. The three-stringed
fingerboard has a soft, ethereal
quality, played mostly in the dulcimer
fretting the melody string and
strumming. The six-stringed
fingerboard has a very clear, strong
resonant property and is designed to be
played with complicated chord
structures. This fingerboard is
overhung and widened so as to permit
extreme bending of the note. The
walnut of the fingerboards is
bookmatched, and the grain pattern
chosen to create a visual sense of
motion. It is taken from the same 4-ft.
block of wood as the sides and back of
the instrument, the block being
re-sawn over and over to get close to
identical grain patterns. The top is
northern red cedar, chosen for its
straight grain and highly valued
accoustical property as well as its visual
tone which comes into harmony with
the rest of the woods used. The
mahogany was taken from the same
section of one tree. Its pulsating grain
accentuates the bold lines
of the walnut and cedar.*"

RICK STONER
Niwot, Colo.
A head of time
Teak, brass
14 x 8 x 8; $750
Photo by Jackson Wolfe

PAUL S. KOPEL
Rochester, N.Y.
Desk/mantel clock
Walnut, acrylic, brass
6-3/8 x 9-3/4 x 3-3/4; $65
Photo by Campbell Photos, Inc.

DOUGLAS W. WALKER
Ouray, Colo.
30-hour wall-hung clock
Cherry, holly
face, 24 x 18; overall height, 46;
$1,150

*"All wood except mirrors inlaid in
back plate and lead enclosed in weight.*

D. H. & G. H. BRETSCHNEIDER
Swarthmore, Pa.
1976 tall case clock
Mahogany
93 high; $1,850
Photo by Donald H. Lee

*"All joinery was done by hand;
finials, rosettes and molding were
handcarved and planed."*

LAWRENCE B. HUNTER
San Diego, Calif.
Clock IV
Black walnut
86 high; great wheel 26 dia.; $3,000

*"...a kinetic sculpture with the
functional basis of a clock."*

DARWIN O. COLLINS
Bettendorf, Iowa
Scrub plane
Maple
2-1/4 x 2 x 9-11/16

ANTHONY J. PUGLIESE
Palo Alto, Calif.
Round bottom plane
Cherry, rosewood
3-1/2 high, 10 long

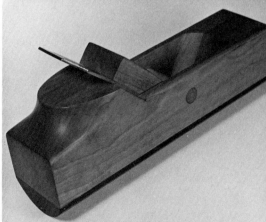

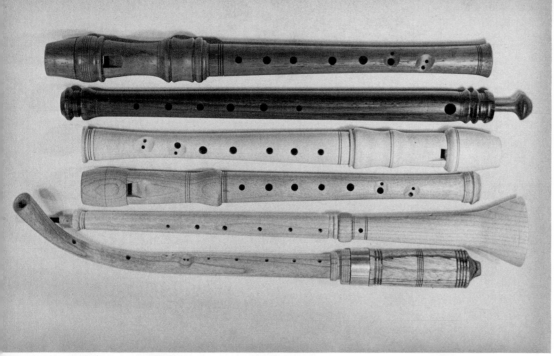

KENT FORRESTER
Murray, Ky.
Krumhorn, musette, recorders and fife
Zebrawood, cherry, maple, cocobolo,
vermilion
longest, 17

M. U. ZAKARIYA
Arlington, Va.
Low-power microscope
Boxwood, cocobolo, cherry, brass,
ivory
18 high; $800

*"The miscoscope has a 2-lens
Huyghens eyepiece and 4 objective
lenses, each in a boxwood nipple,
threaded on the inside. The lenses are
held in place by a boxwood retainer
ring. The eyepiece is composed of 4
turned pieces of cocobolo, each
threaded together to hold the lenses
and diaphragms. It comes apart easily
for cleaning. An adjustable stage is
mounted onto the shaft by threads and
nuts of cocobolo and carries a substage
mirror, spring slide holder, and
specimen tweezer. The base is of
cherry, with hand-planed moldings
and drawer for extra objectives and
slides. This is an original design, based
very loosely on the Marshall type of
microscope of 1725."*

PAT MATHEWS
Eureka, Calif.
Gunstock
Pacific madrone
Photo by T. Nowell

KENNETH M. SCHAEFER
Kirkwood, Mo.
Sliding-cover music movement case
Spruce, black walnut, Plexiglas, brass
Swiss music movement
3-1/4 x 4-3/4 x 14-1/2; $500
Photo by Francis Scheidegger

*"The two covers slide on Formica strips
and can be completely removed for an
unobstructed view of the music
movement."*

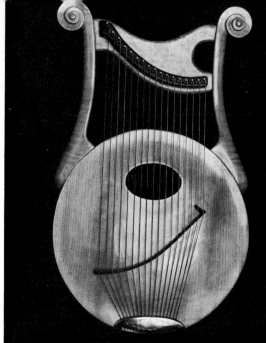

MARTHA L. RISING
No. Hollywood, Calif.
Music stand
Walnut, rosewood
48 x 24; $450

M. G. MALMQUIST
St. Paul, Minn.
Lyre
Fiddleback maple, bird's-eye maple,
ebony, spruce
20 high

*"This is not just a decorative piece for
the wall. It is an eminently playable
instrument, with 17 strings,
tuned chromatically."*

STEVEN W. SORLI
Mineral Point, Wis.
17th-century Italian-style harpsichord
Cypress, basswood, boxwood, walnut
75 x 34; $7,000

STEVE LEVINE
Charlestown, N.H.
Music stand
Red oak
37 x 25; $65

JOHN WATSON
Binghamton, N.Y.
French harpsichord
Poplar, basswood, ebony,
spruce, beech, oak
91 x 36 x 11; $6,500
Photo by Gary Forbes
Soundboard painting by James L. Kie

Toys and Utensils

KEITH A. THOMAS (overleaf)
Alamo, Calif.
Detail: rolling pins

RON TENNEY
Westerville, Ohio
Toy train
Red oak
engine, 8 x 10-1/2 x 19-1/2
tender, 6-1/2 x 6 x 13

HARRY WUNSCH
Westport, Conn.
Dappled jumper
White pine, basswood, beech, walnut,
mahogany, maple
43 x 21 x 57

"Adults too may ride. No metal except
the bolts holding base to rockers."

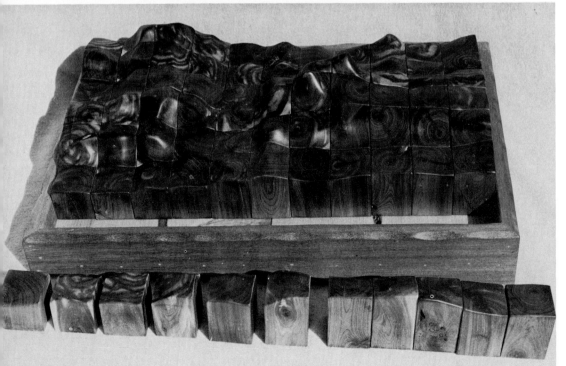

TED BARROW
Del Norte, Colo.
Topographical puzzle
Juniper, mahogany
4 x 18 x 24

"The puzzle was made to use some
scrap pieces left from another project.
They seemed too beautiful to discard.
The box that contains the puzzle was
designed with a taper so that it can
hang on the wall and be enjoyed as
sculpture."

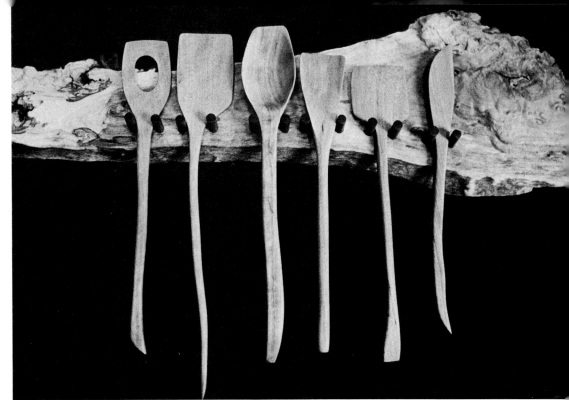

FLETCHER & CAROL COX
Tougaloo, Miss.
*Kitchen utensils and
wall-mounted holder*
Cherry, walnut, pecan
longest utensil, 14; slab, 32

PAUL S. KOPEL
Rochester, N.Y.
Rocking giraffe
Poplar, birch
42 x 14 x 36
Photo by Campbell Photos, Inc.

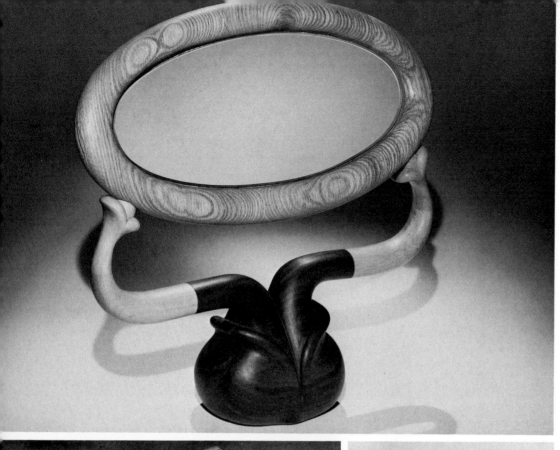

FRANCISCO PEREZ
South Meriden, Conn.
Mirror
Maple, walnut, oak
12-1/2 x 12-1/2

FLETCHER COX
Tougaloo, Miss.
Letter box
Walnut
4-1/2 x 9-1/2 x 12

*"The top is hand carved; the dovetails
are hand cut; the bottom is solid,
floating in the frame."*

JEFFREY S. WARSHAFSKY
Winthrop, Mass.
Sculptured cribbage board
Black walnut
11 x 11 x 2-1/4; $80

JUDI R. BARTHOLOMEW
Milwaukee, Wis.
Woodland chess set
Black walnut, birch; chessboard,
cowhide
king, 4-1/2 high
Photo by Tom Cesel

*"Set includes mushroom pawns,
tree-trunk castles, thistle bishops,
jackrabbit knights and owl kings and
queens. No two pieces are identical;
all are lead-weighted."*

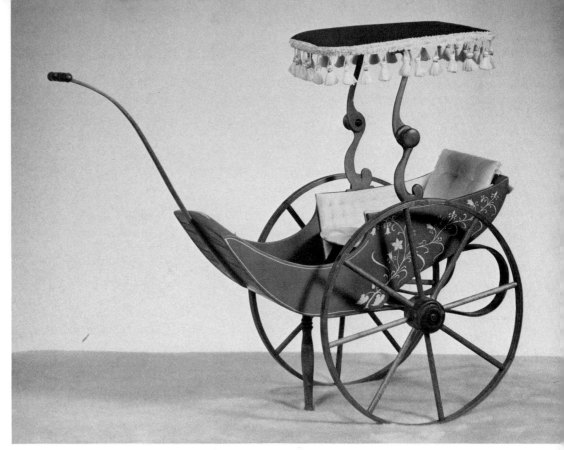

FRANK H. CARMAN
Rochester, N.Y.
Doll carriage
Ash, maple
20 x 7 x 17; $550

"The two-wheel baby carriage was among the earliest used. It was felt to be safer to pull a cart with baby in it than to push it. The carriage body is painted blue with a raised hand-painted bellflower design. The surrey top is a tilt-top. The inside of the carriage is upholstered in quilted white satin."

JOSEPH R. AGNONE
Jackson Heights, N.Y.
Chessboard
Narra, rosewood, bird's-eye maple,
dyed veneers
4 x 19 x 19; $1,500

"Top slides out and reverses to expose chessboard and compartment for gamepieces."

KENT FORRESTER
Murray, Ky.
Marble toy/sculpture
Walnut, cherry, birch, maple, oak
11 x 11 x 25

"A hit on the plunger (top) drives a marble down and around to the cup at the bottom."

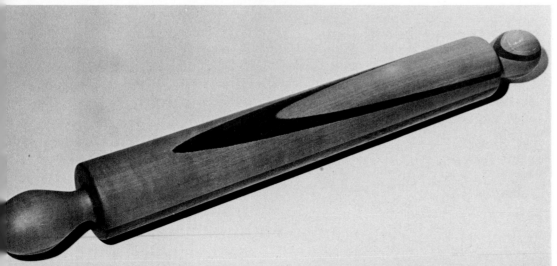

DAVID J. LUTRICK
Seattle, Wash.
Rolling pin
Walnut, cherry, maple
18 long, 2 dia.

DELMAR G. ESAU
Los Angeles, Calif.
Woodroll
Oak
40 x 9-1/2 x 57

"Seven steel balls rest on the top of the
large structure near an opening into
which they are dropped one at a time.
Each ball rolls through a small channel
cut inside the large piece, gathering
momentum and then flying out of the
opening in the lower front of the large
piece (shown plugged in picture).
The ball flies across to the second
piece where it stops inside and then
begins a gentle roll out the other side
down the S-shaped bridge. The ball
then rolls counterclockwise in the
funnel in ever narrowing circles until it
drops down the center, after which it
rolls through the channel and around
in a clockwise direction and comes to
rest in the center of the small area."

GUNTHER KEIL
Rexville, N.Y.
Horse cart with two men
Maple
6-1/2 x 4 x 11; $15

HERBERT EATON &
DENNIS MARTIN
Bloomington, Ill.
Scoopivot
Walnut, maple, oak or cherry
5-1/4 x 5 x 10-1/2; $24
Photo by Ken Kashian

"...an uncomplicated toy that
encourages children to run and
perform fine-motor movements such as
pushing and lifting. The low center of
gravity, due to the extra-wide wheels,
ensures that no matter how fast the
child runs, the toy will not tip over."

EILEEN BANASHEK
Los Angeles, Calif.
Periwinkle and Upstart
Pine, mahogany, maple
Periwinkle, 31 x 15 x 48; $225
Upstart, 27 x 13 x 37; $200

BARNEY P. SMITH
Newark, Ohio
Chess table
Walnut, maple
26 x 19-1/2 x 19-1/2

*"The legs are inverted balusters from
my 100-year-old home which was razed
to make way for a highway."*

JOYCE A. STEPHAN
Lancaster, Pa.
Spoon rack
Walnut
22 x 11 wide

*"Pennsylvania German in design.
Inlaid with bone."*

MARK BALDWIN
Surry, Maine
Bathtub
Cedar, mahogany
$1,000

*"It may be lined with epoxy, or left
plain wood."*

EMMERICH I. OLAH
Phoenix, Ariz.
*Bicentennial Washington memorial
chess set*
Mountain juniper, maple, walnut
figures, 4 to 5; board 24 x 24; $5,000

CHARLES E. BIRD
Holly Hill, Fla.
Backgammon board
Walnut, mahogany, purpleheart,
poplar burl, padauk, zebrano, holly
rosewood, cherry
playing surface, 20 x 20
closed, 13-1/2 x 21

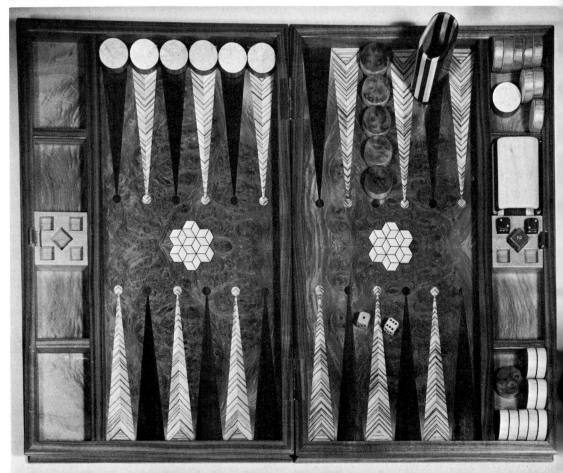

CYNTHIA BELISLE
Rochester, N.Y.
Mirror wall piece
Cherry
17 x 22-1/2 x 3-3/4

JOHN DODD
Rochester, N.Y.
Rocking swan
Oak
32 x 22 x 36

JOHN W. MUDD
Kentfield, Calif.
Carousel horse
Cherry, vermilion, birch, poplar,
brass, wool
43 x 29-1/2

JOHN WHITEHEAD
Portland, Ore.
Salad utensils
Teak
12 long; $32.50 pr.

SHARON D. SPRAGUE
Bloomington, Ind.
Puzzles
Poplar
8-1/4 x 7 x 1-1/4; $7.50
Photo by Talbot Studio

UOSIS JUODVALKIS
Providence, R.I.
Knife rack
Birch plywood
3 x 10 x 4

KEITH A. THOMAS
Alamo, Calif.
Rolling pin
Wenge, angico, pau

CHESTER KNIGHT
Houston, Tex.
Butter mold
Black walnut
5 high, 2-1/2 dia.

THOMAS B. PRIETO
Columbus, Ohio
Hand mirror
Walnut, maple, mother-of-pearl
mirror, 6-3/4 dia.; handle, 7 long
Photo by C. Selkow

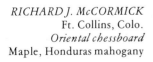

RICHARD J. McCORMICK
Ft. Collins, Colo.
Oriental chessboard
Maple, Honduras mahogany

*"The woods were left in their natural
color. No veneers were used; each
piece had to be mitered and joined at
very low tolerances. The side molds
were rough-shaped on a radial arm saw
with many passes through the blade,
which was set at a different height
each pass."*

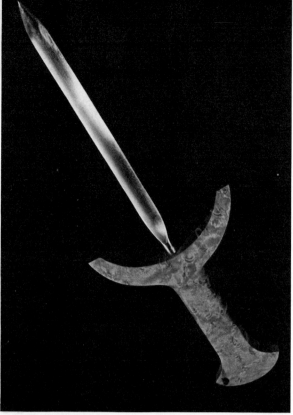

AMIL ST. AUGUSTINE
Novato, Calif.
Cheval glass
Koa
60 x 30 x 21 ; $800

DONALD JORDAN CRAIG
Plattsburgh, N.Y.
Ceremonial dagger
Bird's-eye maple, stainless steel blade
16 long

ROBERT T. HARGRAVE
Cambridge, Mass.
Odalisque mirror
Fir plywood
24 dia. ; $85

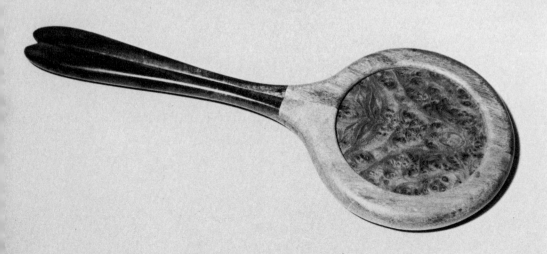

CURTIS MINIER
Seattle, Wash.
Hand mirror
Koa, elm burl
16 long, 6-1/2 dia. ; $45
Photo by Joan Sisson

MICHEL & CAROLE PEPIN
Co. Megantic, Quebec, Canada
Dog-faced toy truck
Pine, leather
7 x 18; $40

FRED M. ADAMS
Shreveport, La.
Nutcracker
Maple, poplar
5 x 9 x 16; $25
Photo by Thurman C. Smith

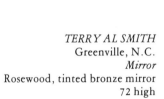

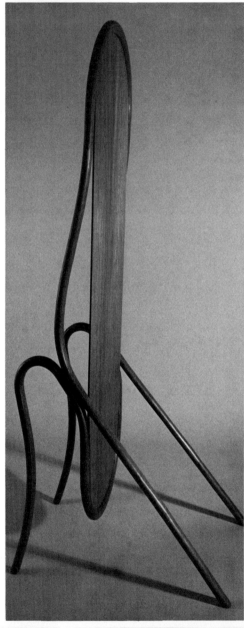

TERRY AL SMITH
Greenville, N.C.
Mirror
Rosewood, tinted bronze mirror
72 high

GLENN ADOLPH GAUVRY
Philadelphia, Pa.
Floor-standing mirror
Laminated cherry veneer, cherry
veneer backing (1/28)
66 high

DAVID HOFFMAN
Ithaca, N.Y.
Shaker-style rolling pin
Black cherry, cherry
21 long; $24

C. R. JOHNSON
Stoughton, Wis.
Rocking beast #2
Mahogany, leather
36 x 22 x 26; $350

MARK DAVIS
Rhinelander, Wis.
Wooden crane
White and yellow birch, oak
boom, 22 long
cab, 11 high x 6 wide; $125

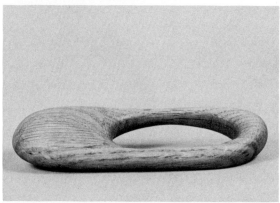

THOMAS P. NEWCOMB
Rochester, N.Y.
Backgammon set
Walnut, spalted curly maple
closed, 3 x 9 x 18

PETER C. HEITZEBERG
Los Gatos, Calif.
Baby rattle
White oak
1/2 x 4-7/8 x 1-3/4; $45
Photo by James Heitzeberg

"The delicate soft tone is created by seven kernels of corn held within the cavity of each rattle. The rattle was baby tested and the shape was easy to hold and nice to chew on."

RONALD GAUTHIER
Quebec, Quebec, Canada
Sugar bowl
Cedar
$35

ROBERT F. STREET
Aberdeen, Wash.
Salt shaker and pepper mill
Teak
8-3/4 x 2-7/8 dia.
Photo by Jones Photo Co.

DAVID N. EBNER
Brookhaven, N.Y.
Rocking horse
Douglas fir, German yellow
pine, hemp
36 x 24 x 48

Index